# The Down & Up Fall

This edition is published by special arrangement with Morrow Junior Books,
a division of William Morrow & Company, Inc.

Grateful acknowledgment is made to Morrow Junior Books, a division of William Morrow &
Company, Inc. for permission to reprint *The Down & Up Fall* by Johanna Hurwitz, illustrated
by Gail Owens. Text copyright © 1996 by
Johanna Hurwitz; illustrations copyright © 1996 by Gail Owens.

Printed in the United States of America

ISBN   0-15-314366-5

4   5 6   7   8   9   10    060    03   02   01

Johanna Hurwitz

# The Down & Up Fall

illustrated by Gail Owens

 Harcourt

Orlando    Boston    Dallas    Chicago    San Diego

Visit *The Learning Site!*

**www.harcourtschool.com**

*In memory of Pam Conrad—*
*"It is not often that someone comes along*
*who is a true friend and a good writer."*

# Contents

# 1
# Together Again

On the first Wednesday in September, Bolivia Raab woke with a start. For a fraction of a moment she didn't know where she was. Then she smiled to herself. She wasn't in her bedroom at home in Ithaca, New York. Instead she was in the guest room of her great-aunt and -uncle in Woodside, New Jersey. Unlike her previous visits with her relatives, when she never stayed more than a few weeks, she was now going to be there a really long time. In fact, during the coming six months, while her parents were away in Turkey on an archeological dig, Bolivia would even attend the local school.

Bolivia jumped out of bed and pulled off the towel covering a tall birdcage near the window.

"Good morning," she greeted Lucette, the bright green parrot inside the cage.

"Good morning. Have a nice day," squawked the bird.

"I think I will," Bolivia told the parrot. "Rory and Derek and I are all going to be in sixth grade together at Woodside Middle School. And it's a new school for them, just like it is for me. Their old school only went up to fifth grade."

"Roryderek," Lucette called out in triumph. "Roryderek."

It had taken many, many weeks for Bolivia to teach her parrot the names of the two boys who were her friends here in Woodside.

Because she was not the sort of girl who spent a lot of time bothering over her looks, Bolivia didn't worry about what to wear. She just dug a clean T-shirt and some underwear out of the still half-packed trunk in the corner of the room. Then she pulled on the jeans that she had worn the day before and quickly combed her red hair into a ponytail.

Bolivia checked. There was still plenty of food in the cage to keep Lucette happy during the day.

She removed the little water dish from the cage and went into the bathroom to refill it with fresh cold water.

"Good-bye, Lucette. I'll see you this afternoon," she promised the parrot.

"Good morning. Have a nice day," the bird said. She had a rather limited vocabulary, and this was her usual morning message.

"Thanks, Lucette. I'll need all the good wishes I can get," said Bolivia. She wouldn't have admitted it to a soul, but she was a little nervous about going off to a new school. She took a deep breath and went downstairs. She was ready to face Woodside Middle School.

"First you've got to eat a good breakfast," Mrs. Golding insisted.

"Oh, Aunt Sophie. I don't think I could eat all this. Not even half of it," said Bolivia, looking at the eggs and toast waiting for her on the table.

"Just eat a little then," Mrs. Golding pleaded. "You don't want to get hungry before lunchtime."

Bolivia sat down and bit into a slice of toast. A moment later she heard a loud banging at the front door.

"I believe that your escorts are here," Mrs. Golding said, heading to the entranceway.

Sure enough, she came back followed by Rory and Derek.

"Wow!" commented Bolivia when she saw her two friends.

Both boys were wearing new jeans and freshly ironed sport shirts. Rory's dark hair was parted on the side and slicked down. There had been an obvious attempt to do the same to Derek's blond hair, but its natural curl was already taking over. They both had on white sneakers that were so clean that Bolivia could tell they were brand-new.

"You both look like you'd glow in the dark," remarked Bolivia, looking them over. "I hardly recognize you."

"They look very handsome," said Mrs. Golding, beaming at the two boys.

"The girls are probably all going to fall for you the way you look now," Bolivia teased them. "Of course, they don't know what you're really like."

Derek made a face. "We thought we should kind of dress up a bit on the first day," he said, blushing. "We'll be our old grungy selves again by tomorrow."

4

Bolivia sniffed Rory's hair. "Wow. The gook on your hair smells like a botanical garden."

Rory rubbed his head and smelled his hand. "I told my mother I hate this stuff," he complained.

"You look wonderful," Mrs. Golding insisted. "Bolivia, maybe you should change into a nicer-looking shirt," she suggested.

"I'm not changing," Bolivia said adamantly. "This is the real me that you see before you. Take it or leave it!"

"It's okay. You look fine," Rory said, laughing. "Besides, I wouldn't be so *presumptuous* as to comment on your appearance."

"There you go again, using your big words," said Bolivia. She swallowed some milk and stood up from the table. Rory's father taught English at their new school. She wondered if she would get him as a teacher. "If your dad teaches all his students to talk like that, we're all going to have to walk around lugging huge dictionaries so we can understand one another."

Rory ignored this remark. He pushed his glasses up on his nose. "I still can't believe that you're actually coming to school with us and staying until the spring. It's fantastic."

"Yeah," Derek agreed. He looked at his watch. "Come on. We don't want to miss the bus," he said.

"My dad offered to give us a ride," Rory explained as they walked toward the door. "But we've been looking forward to taking the bus. Besides, my dad always goes to school really early."

Bolivia gave her aunt a hug and followed the boys out the door. Mr. Golding was in front, cutting the grass on the small lawn. "Have a good time," he called to the three students.

"A good time?" asked Rory. "We're going to school, not a baseball game."

"These are the best years of your lives," Mr. Golding reminded him.

"That's easy for him to say," commented Derek as they walked to the bus stop. "He won't have to do any homework tonight."

"Or study for tests," added Rory.

"Do you think we might be in the same homeroom?" Bolivia asked.

"There's going to be a mob of kids," Rory pointed out. "The sixth grade is made up of all of last year's fifth graders from our old school and classes that went to Hillside Elementary and Brookside Elementary too."

"Gosh. We'll probably be making a lot of new friends then," said Bolivia.

"Hey," said Rory, "we don't need more friends. We've got each other. That's plenty."

"Wait a minute," said Bolivia. "It's true I'm your friend, but I don't exactly *belong* to you." She always forgot, when she wasn't in his company for a while, how Rory had a tendency to be demanding and possessive. He liked to dominate situations. The problem was that Bolivia liked to take over too. So even though they were good friends, there could be personality clashes between them. Bolivia looked over at Derek. He was very easygoing. He'd agree to anything Rory told him.

As if Rory had read her thoughts, he said now, "Today you'll sit next to me on the bus. Tomorrow you can sit next to Derek."

"Hold it," Bolivia said as the bus pulled up at the corner where they were waiting. She was about to protest that she could sit wherever she wanted. However, when they boarded the bus, every window seat was taken. That meant there were only single seats left. Contrary to Rory's plan, the three friends each had to sit next to somebody else.

"Hi," Bolivia greeted the girl she found herself next to.

"Hi," the girl responded. "Is this your first day at middle school too?"

"Yep. And I bet I've come farther than anyone else."

"I've already been on this bus for twenty minutes. I got on at the very first stop, so you can't be coming from farther away than me," Bolivia's seatmate told her.

"But I took an airplane from Ithaca yesterday," said Bolivia. "You can't beat that."

"Ithaca? Where's that?" asked the girl, looking puzzled.

"There's a Greek island named Ithaca, and there's a town in Michigan named Ithaca, but I come from Ithaca, New York."

"You know," said the girl, "I heard that kids came from all over town to this school, but I didn't know that they came from other *states* too."

"I'm just here for a few months," Bolivia explained. She had to raise her voice to make herself heard. All around her kids were talking to classmates they hadn't seen since last June. Bolivia looked to where Rory was sitting. He was working hard trying to carry on a conversation with Derek, who was several seats away.

"Middle school is going to be neat," Bolivia's companion said. "We're going to have different teachers for every subject. There's a huge gym for phys ed. And I'm taking Spanish. What foreign language are you taking?"

"German," Bolivia told her.

"Most kids are choosing French or Spanish, but I have a friend who's also taking German."

"I guess I like to be different," Bolivia said. She knew that Rory and Derek had selected Spanish as their foreign language, just like the girl sitting beside her.

"Do you play an instrument?" the girl asked.

"No. Do you?"

"I just started taking clarinet lessons last spring. If they think I'm good enough, maybe I can be in the school band."

"We're here!" a voice called out, and some of the kids began booing as the bus pulled into the school's driveway. They might be booing, Bolivia thought, but they certainly seemed eager to get off the bus. She and her seatmate were jostled to the front. Once outside, Bolivia waited for Rory and Derek so they could walk together.

"My name's Bolivia. What's yours?" she asked the girl.

"DeDe. DeDe Rawson."

"I'll look for you," Bolivia told DeDe.

"Come on," Rory called, and he pulled Bolivia along toward the school entrance. She remembered what he'd said about their not needing new friends. Well, he was wrong about that. You could never have too many friends, and that girl, DeDe, seemed like she'd be fun. Bolivia realized that his teachers weren't the only ones who were going to teach Rory a few new things this fall.

September 3

Dear Mom and Dad,

The school here is humongous! It's not as big as the university where you teach, but to see 1,000 students rushing about from class to class is wild! They could use some traffic lights and cops in the hallways.

I thought I might be in the same homeroom as Rory and Derek, but it turns out that we're in three separate rooms. We also have different teachers for each of our subjects: math, English, social studies, foreign language, gym, music, and art.

None of us got Rory's father for English. I bet he arranged that. It could be embarrassing for him to have to scold one of us if we did something silly in class. And imagine if Rory raised his hand to speak and said, *"Dad!"*

The teachers I do have all seem great, but you usually don't find out what a teacher is really like on the first day of school. I guess teachers, like kids, are on their best behavior at the beginning.

My homeroom teacher (Mrs. Jansen) gave out a list of afterschool activities that will begin in a couple of weeks. On Tuesdays and Thursdays there are special clubs that you can sign up for. Some are sports like field hockey and swimming. Other activities include a nature club, a choral singing group (that's the one I think I'd like to join), a journalism club that produces the school magazine, a cycling club, a class to learn sign language, a cooking club, and a load of others too.

I keep remembering the great concert we went to at the university last spring. Remember? We heard Haydn's *Creation*. All those voices singing that beautiful music was like listening to angels. I would like to be standing in the middle of the singers and adding to the sound.

> Love from your
> would-be angel,
> Bolivia

P.S. On the bus going to school, I sat next to a girl named DeDe. She seemed nice. I hope we can get to be friends.

# 2
# Settling Down

Amazingly, within two days a pattern was set. It was almost as if someone had written it down in ink. Each morning, no matter how early Bolivia woke and ate breakfast, Rory and Derek were already up, dressed, fed, and at the door waiting for her. Bolivia couldn't believe that neither boy ever overslept. She suspected that they skimped on or even skipped breakfast at home, since they were so quick to grab the homemade muffin or slice of toast that her aunt always offered.

Every morning the three friends walked together to the bus stop. Right away, it was clear to Bolivia that Rory and Derek expected her to sit with one of them if there was a rare double empty seat. On other days they would each find an empty seat wherever they could.

The Friday of the first week of school Bolivia managed to sit together with DeDe again.

"How's it going?" Bolivia asked as she sat down. "Do you like middle school?"

"It's fun," DeDe said cheerfully. "Of course, I forgot my locker combination yesterday. I spent fifteen minutes turning one of the numbers to the left instead of the right, and another one right instead of left. I felt like an idiot. But now I think I've mastered it. And I love having so many different teachers."

DeDe had such an upbeat attitude that Bolivia really liked her. She was sorry that she never saw her during the school day.

"I'm busy this weekend," said Bolivia. "But maybe we could do something together next Saturday or Sunday. How about it?"

"Next weekend? No, I'm going to be away," said DeDe.

"Oh. All weekend?" asked Bolivia.

"Yeah." DeDe blushed and turned her head away.

Bolivia wondered if her seatmate was telling the truth. Maybe she just didn't want to become friends with her.

DeDe turned her head back to face Bolivia. "My parents are divorced," she explained. "That's why I'm going to be busy next weekend. I'll be visiting my father."

"Oh, sure," said Bolivia, understanding the situation. It must be awful to have divorced parents, she thought. Even though her own parents were thousands of miles away, she felt a lot luckier than DeDe. "Maybe we can do something the Saturday after next," she said.

"Great," said DeDe, nodding with enthusiasm.

"Hey, are you going to sign up for any of the afterschool groups?" Bolivia asked DeDe. Maybe they could join something together.

"I've been practicing my clarinet like mad," said DeDe, laughing. "In fact, I'm driving my mother up the wall. She says other mothers have to yell at their kids to practice, and she has to yell at me to stop. I hope I'm good enough to join the band."

"I like music too," Bolivia said. "I don't play an instrument. But I'd like to join the choral group."

Bolivia didn't tell DeDe that she'd had a big argument with Rory and Derek the day before on the subject of afterschool activities.

"We're not signing up for anything," Rory had decreed when Bolivia mentioned the choral group.

"What do you mean, 'We're not signing up for anything'?" she had asked him. "I can sign up for anything I want."

"If we stay after school for any of those clubs, then we can't get our homework done. We'll have to do it after supper. And that means we'll probably miss our favorite television programs," Rory explained.

"Television? You mean you're going to let TV run your life?" asked Bolivia in amazement. "I don't watch it at home, and I'm not planning to sit around watching it here in Woodside either."

"You don't have to watch TV if you don't want to," said Derek, trying to calm her down. "But you know, there are some good educational programs you could look at. And besides, it's more fun when we all do our homework together," he reminded her.

"Yes, it is," Bolivia said. The three of them had sat together doing their work. "But that doesn't mean we have to do it together *every single day*. We could pick one day when we'd each join a club. There must be something you'd like from the big choice that they give. Anyhow, even if you guys don't sign up for anything, I'm joining the choral group."

"What's the big deal about the choral group?" Rory wanted to know. "If you want to sing, go ahead and sing to us."

"Sure," said Bolivia sarcastically. "I'll start singing out here in the middle of the street, and they'll lock me up for being crazy."

"Don't you want to spend your afternoons with us?" Derek asked her. "We thought that was why you're spending this time in Woodside instead of in Turkey with your parents. So we could be together."

Derek had looked so downcast that Bolivia felt a little guilty. Still, it seemed foolish not to take advantage of the afterschool programs. After all, there were seven days in the week, and she was talking about going off on her own for only an hour and a half.

"Nine to three is enough school for me," Rory proclaimed.

"Yeah." Derek agreed with his friend. Bolivia wondered if Derek ever disagreed with anything Rory said.

Disgusted, she stopped arguing for the time being. It was hard to convince Rory of anything. When he made up his mind about something, it was like talking to a rock.

Derek's father, who was a dentist, sometimes worked on Saturdays. But when he didn't, he often took Rory and Derek somewhere. Now Bolivia was added to the group.

It was raining the first Saturday of September, so Dr. Curry decided it was a good day to drive into New York City with the three kids. They spent the entire day at the American Museum of Natural History, looking at exhibits and viewing a special nature film. They even ate lunch in the museum's large cafeteria. In the gift shop Bolivia bought a few postcards to send to her friends back in Ithaca.

"We haven't been to the planetarium in ages," Derek commented on the way home. "Next time we should go there."

"Good idea," his father said. "We'll do that if it's raining again. But if the weather is good, I thought we'd go to Hicks's Orchard and pick apples. Your mother wants to come along too."

"Great," said Rory. He turned to Bolivia. "We went there last fall. It's loads of fun picking all those apples."

"Mmm. And afterward my mom made applesauce and the world's best apple pie," said Derek, licking his lips.

Bolivia laughed. She'd enjoyed the day very much. Unlike her friends, she'd never been to the natural history museum before. The place had so many exhibits that you could spend a week inside and probably not see everything. She knew she was lucky to have a chance to be able to do neat stuff with Rory and Derek on the weekends. Still, she wished that all her time weren't going to be arranged for her. How could she ever get to make other friends if she spent every single moment with the same two boys?

Now Rory and Derek would be expecting her to go apple picking with them in two weeks.

Suddenly Bolivia remembered that she had made a date with DeDe for the Saturday after next. She knew what she'd do. She'd ask DeDe if she wanted to come along. Derek's father drove a station wagon, so there'd be enough room in the car, and she was sure he wouldn't object. Bolivia looked at Rory and Derek. How they would react to this extra passenger was of course another matter.

Dear Mom and Dad,

How are you, and how is the dig? Did you find anything spectacular yet, or is it just dirt, dirt, dirt?

I'm fine. Aunt Sophie and Uncle Lou are fine too. And so are Rory and Derek and their families. I see a lot of them (Rory and Derek, that is) because we go to school together every day and we also do our homework together in the afternoons.

I have one problem, though, and I need your help. I want to join one of those after-school clubs. The problem is that neither Rory or Derek wants to stay after three o'clock. That part is okay with me. I don't need them following after me every moment. However, that's not the way Aunt Sophie and Uncle Lou feel. They say they'd worry about me staying late at school if the boys weren't with me. Isn't that crazy? They don't seem to realize that you both let me do all sorts of things on my own back home. I'm not a baby!

Since I can't seem to change Rory's and Derek's minds about staying after school, and I haven't managed to convince Aunt Sophie and Uncle Lou to let me stay, this is what I want you to do: Please, please, please write a letter to them real fast. Tell them I should be allowed to stay late one day a week. They'll listen to you even if they won't listen to me.

Love & hugs,
Bolivia

# 3

# Inside the
# Window Well

One afternoon a few days later Rory was scheduled to go for an eye exam. Mrs. Dunn invited Bolivia to come along for the ride. Rory's little sister, Edna, and Derek were getting into the car.

"No, thanks," Bolivia said. "I think I'll stick around here this afternoon."

"Oh, please," begged Edna. "I love you *this* much," she said, holding out her arms to show the amount of her affection for Bolivia.

"I love you too," Bolivia told Edna, and blew her a kiss. She thought it would be neat to have a cute little sister like that. But Bolivia also liked the idea of a couple of hours on her own without Rory giving her orders. He was so bossy that he even said things like "We'll do our math homework first" when the three of them studied together.

"Why can't I do my social studies assignment before the math?" Bolivia demanded.

"Aw, let's all do the math," said Derek, predictably.

When the car drove off, Bolivia went into the house. "Where's Uncle Lou?" she asked her aunt.

"He went for a haircut," her aunt told her.

"Is there anything I can do to help out?" Bolivia offered.

"Why, that's awfully thoughtful of you," said Mrs. Golding. "Actually I've got some boxes of old clothing in the basement," she commented. "I was planning to take everything to the Salvation Army tomorrow. Could you bring the boxes upstairs for me?" she asked.

"Sure," said Bolivia. "I'll get them right now."

In all the time Bolivia had spent with the Goldings, she couldn't remember being in the basement more than once or twice, when she helped with the laundry. She'd always been in a hurry to complete her chore, and she'd never explored the area. Now she looked around. The basement was not finished, and the dim lighting didn't encourage anyone to stay. There was a shelf with Mr. Golding's tools, and there was some old furniture. Bolivia found a few cartons and guessed they were the ones her aunt had been referring to.

As she lifted the top box, she heard a funny scratching sort of noise. Mice didn't frighten Bolivia, but she was curious. She walked toward the source of the noise and found herself standing near one of the walls where there was a window well. The actual window was so dirty that it was almost impossible to see out of it. But Bolivia was certain that this was where the sound was coming from. She listened carefully, and sure enough, she heard something scratching against the glass.

Bolivia ran upstairs and asked her aunt for a flashlight.

"Can't you see down there?" questioned her aunt. "The boxes are on an old table."

"I found the boxes, but there's something else I can't see very well," said Bolivia. She was so puzzled by her discovery that she had forgotten about the old clothing she had gone downstairs for.

She took the flashlight from her aunt and returned to the basement. At the foot of the stairs she listened for a moment. Yes, the sounds were still coming from the same area. She hurried over to the window well and turned on the flashlight. Staring at her from the other side of the dirty window were four pairs of eyes belonging to a litter of kittens. It was an amazing discovery.

Bolivia charged up the stairs. "Come. Look what I found," she called out excitedly.

"What is it?" asked Mrs. Golding, heading toward the basement steps.

"No, no. Outdoors. Come."

The older woman followed Bolivia outside. "What is it?" she asked again, puzzled by Bolivia's excitement. "Why are we going outside?"

Bolivia rushed to the window well and removed the heavy plastic cover that protected it. Instantly the kittens scrambled into the far corner, where they huddled together. Bolivia pointed to the mass of gray and white and black fur. "Look!" she shouted. "Look what I found!"

"Oh, my heavens!" gasped Mrs. Golding. "How do you think they got there?"

"Aren't they darling?" asked Bolivia, bending down to get a closer look at the kittens.

"Keep away from them," her aunt scolded.

"They're dirty. I bet they have fleas too. I don't want you getting scratched and infected," she told her niece.

"They're so tiny," cooed Bolivia, ignoring Mrs. Golding's anxiety. "They're just darling. I wonder where their mother is. I bet she's that old black-and-white stray cat I saw running across the lawn the other day. She must have given birth to the kittens right here." It was amazing to think that such a thing had taken place without her or her aunt or uncle realizing it. "Maybe the kittens are hungry," Bolivia added in an afterthought.

"As soon as your uncle gets back, he'll know what to do," Mrs. Golding said. "We can't let them stay here. We'll have to take them to the animal shelter or something."

"Oh, Aunt Sophie! We can't just remove them from here," Bolivia objected. "Their mother is going to come looking for them." She put her arms around her aunt. "Their mother picked this window well as the safest spot she could find for her babies. If we move them, she won't know where they are."

"Then she picked the wrong place," said Mrs. Golding. "I don't want those dirty things here. Before you know it, they'll be old enough to have kittens of their own. And soon this place will be a mass of stray kittens. Do you know that just today I heard on the radio that one female cockroach gives birth to forty million cockroaches in only two years!"

"Cockroaches? But these are kittens!" Bolivia protested. "There's no way you'd have forty million kittens."

"Well, no. I guess you're right," said Mrs. Golding. "But I still don't want them here."

"If we keep the plastic cover off the window well, perhaps the kittens will just go away," said Bolivia. But she was only stalling for time. She didn't really think the little creatures were big enough to climb out of the deep well.

"Or maybe their mother will come and remove them," said her aunt hopefully.

Bolivia realized that this was a much more likely possibility.

"I do wish your uncle would hurry and get back. He'll be amazed at what's happened."

"Yeah. I can't wait till Rory and Derek come back," Bolivia said. "They're in for a big surprise too."

Bolivia moved the plastic cover to the window well still farther off to the side. "I guess the mother cat squeezed her way underneath this," she thought aloud.

Mrs. Golding went into the house, and Bolivia looked for a corner where she could station herself. She wanted to watch in case the mother cat came for her babies.

Twenty minutes passed very, very slowly, and there was no sign of the mother cat. From where she stood, Bolivia could see the opening of the window well, but she couldn't see the kittens. Finally, feeling chilly and stiff, she went into the house.

"I'm going to wash the inside of the basement window so I can see better," she told her aunt. It would be like television to observe the cats through the window, Bolivia thought. Then she smiled to herself. For a person who made a point of not watching television, she realized it was a funny comparison.

The kittens were aware of the activity on the other side of the glass, and they struggled to get as far away from the window as they could. Bolivia watched them with fascination. Poor little things,

31

she thought. If they had been born in the window well, as she was certain they had, then she and Aunt Sophie were the first humans they had ever seen. They must look like strange and horrible giant monsters to the tiny animals.

In a little while Bolivia was joined in the basement by Uncle Lou. "I see you made a big discovery while I was at the barbershop," he said, looking through the window at the ball of fur that was the four kittens huddled together.

"They're so darling," Bolivia told him. "Could I take some food out for the mother? I think she's nursing the babies."

"Well, your aunt and I don't really want to encourage stray cats to come to our yard," her uncle began. But seeing the expression on Bolivia's face, he seemed to reconsider. "I guess it can't hurt to feed her just once. But eventually we'll have to take the kittens to the animal shelter. They'll know what to do with them there."

"Oh, Uncle Lou, that's wonderful!" Bolivia threw her arms around her uncle in her delight at his agreement to put out some food for the cats. She ignored his comment about the animal shelter.

"Remember, we're just feeding the mother cat today," Mr. Golding reminded Bolivia. "We're not going to do it every day."

"I know. I know," Bolivia said. She'd worry about tomorrow's food tomorrow.

September 15

Dear Mom & Dad,

The most absolutely super thing happened this afternoon! I discovered four tiny kittens in the window well on one side of Aunt Sophie's house. It was a total surprise. None of us was the least bit aware of them. They must have been born right there.

When Rory's little sister, Edna, saw them, she got so excited she forgot the word *kittens*. She called them *puppy cats*. Isn't that cute?

I've named them Eeny, Meeny, Miney, and Moe. But I haven't even decided yet which is which.

Aunt Sophie is worried that the kittens are dirty and have germs, but so far, even though they are very small, they are so fierce that I can't touch them. So she doesn't have to worry. If I can't get near them, I can't catch anything.

At first she and Uncle Lou said I could only leave some food for the mother today and tomorrow the kittens would have to go. But I was really hoping that they could stay here longer. By suppertime they agreed to let them remain for a week or so. Besides, Uncle Lou's big hobby is photography and he's already taken a whole roll of film. He kept snapping the shutter again and again and again. I never saw anyone use up film so quickly. He says that's the way professional photographers work. They take hundreds of pictures in order to get the perfect shot. He hopes to be able to photograph the kittens when their mother returns to nurse them.

Right now Uncle Lou is in his darkroom developing the pictures. Maybe I'll be able to send one in my next letter.

Love from Eeny, Meeny,
Miney, Moe, & Bolivia

P.S. Love from Lucette too. She's settled in just fine here.

# 4

# An Apple a Day

Rory and Derek were as excited as Bolivia was over the discovery of the kittens.

"I never saw kittens that were so young and tiny," Rory exclaimed in amazement when he looked at them for the first time.

"They're the same size as my hamster, Hamlet," Derek commented.

Bolivia was glad that the boys shared her pleasure in the kittens, especially since Aunt Sophie and Uncle Lou had mixed feelings about them. But that's what friendship was all about: sharing your good news and bad, sharing your excitement and discoveries.

Unfortunately Rory and Derek were much less pleased with the news that Bolivia wanted to bring

DeDe along when they went to the apple orchard on Saturday. In fact, they were downright annoyed.

"I asked your father, and he said it was fine with him," Bolivia told Derek. "He said the car is big enough for all of us and all the apples we pick too."

"But we didn't pick her to come along. We don't even *know* her," Rory complained.

"Look," Bolivia said, shrugging her shoulders, "if you don't want DeDe to come along, she won't. She and I can do something on our own."

"But we're looking forward to having *you* with us," Derek said.

"Yes, but not DeDe," Rory added.

"It's up to you to decide. DeDe and I can join you or not," Bolivia said to the boys. It would be a little embarrassing to tell DeDe that they weren't going apple picking after all. Still, if that was what Rory and Derek wanted, that was what would happen.

"My father said it was okay," Derek hesitantly reminded Rory. And for once it seemed that Rory was not going to get his way.

\* \* \*

Bolivia thought ahead to Saturday. She loved apples: McIntosh, Macoun, red and yellow Delicious, green Granny Smiths, and every other variety that she could think of. She also liked apple picking, having gone two years before on a class trip to an orchard. Still, she was a little nervous about the Saturday outing. It probably would have been better to spend her first afterschool date with DeDe alone and not together with Rory and Derek.

The two boys were her best friends. Still, there were things about them that she couldn't understand. They did everything together. Everything. They were like Siamese twins, for heaven's sake. Rory never wanted to do anything without Derek at his side. Why didn't Derek ever go off and do something on his own? The two boys had been best friends forever and ever, and now that she was accepted by them, it was expected that she would want to do everything with them too. Why did they assume that? Twins were bad enough. Whoever heard of Siamese triplets?

The crazy thing was that last spring, when the two boys had come to visit her, Rory had protested because she had made all the plans for the week without consulting them. Now that was exactly what he and Derek were doing here in Woodside.

Yet it was also more than that. It was almost as if the boys felt she belonged to them. They weren't willing to let her make more friends because they didn't want to share her with anyone else. They didn't want her to go places without them. They seemed to feel that the time she spent in Woodside was their time and she could use it only under their supervision.

What was worse, her aunt and uncle accepted this situation as natural. On a couple of occasions Bolivia tried to explain to her aunt that she wanted some time to herself. She felt as if she were suffocating. She needed the kind of freedom and space that she was accustomed to having at home.

"Those boys are crazy about you," commented Mrs. Golding on Friday evening. "Ever since the summer you spent here in Woodside, they never stopped talking about you. Whenever they saw me, they always asked if you were coming back. And now you're here. It's just perfect."

"What's perfect?" asked Uncle Lou, coming out

of the small bathroom he used for a darkroom. He had already taken three rolls of pictures of the kittens.

"It's perfect that Bolivia has two such wonderful and loyal friends as Rory and Derek nearby," she said.

Uncle Lou nodded in agreement. He was a quiet man and spent a lot of time locked up with his photographic equipment. You'd think he'd understand that she needed a private space too, Bolivia thought.

Still, it was a small victory on her part that DeDe was coming apple picking, Bolivia thought as she waited for DeDe to arrive that Saturday morning. They were departing for the orchard at nine o'clock, so she'd told DeDe to try to get to the Goldings' house by eight-thirty. She wanted at least a few minutes alone with her new friend.

"Aren't they fantastic?" she asked DeDe as she showed off Eeny, Meeny, Miney, and Moe.

"I have a confession," said DeDe. "I'm a dog person. You'll have to come over to my house sometime and meet my dog, Cookie. But you're right. These kittens are darling." DeDe bent down to get a closer look. The action frightened the kittens, and they hissed at her.

"I have a friend who has a cat and two dogs. In fact, my friend is crazy about all animals. Could we come over together one day after school?"

"Sure," said Bolivia. She was delighted that even before they spent one morning together, DeDe was already planning another visit.

"What's going to happen to the kittens?" DeDe asked.

"I want to keep them here as long as possible," Bolivia said. "But I guess we'll have to take them to an animal shelter one of these days. My aunt isn't as crazy about them as I am."

"Too bad," said DeDe. "I think they destroy them at the animal shelter."

"Destroy? You mean, kill them?" Bolivia was shocked.

DeDe nodded. "Maybe I'm wrong," she said, trying to make Bolivia feel better. "I'm probably wrong about that."

"Of course you're wrong," Bolivia insisted. "A shelter is a place for protection. They wouldn't harm the kittens there."

Promptly at nine o'clock Derek's father pulled his car out of his driveway and to the front of the Golding house. Bolivia and DeDe called good-bye to the Goldings and went to get into the car.

"This is DeDe—" Bolivia started to introduce her friend to Derek's parents.

"Hi, Dr. Curry!" DeDe called out in recognition before Bolivia could even complete the introductions. "He's my dentist!" she exclaimed. She made a grimace so that everyone had a good view of the braces Dr. Curry had put on her teeth.

"No kidding?" said Derek, who was sitting in the backseat. He smiled proudly.

Bolivia and DeDe slid into the backseat next to the boys.

"They say an apple a day keeps the doctor away," DeDe reminded the occupants of the car. "But I see it doesn't keep the dentist away."

Bolivia and Derek laughed.

"What's so funny about that?" asked Rory.

Bolivia could see he wasn't in the best of moods this morning. "Did you know there are about two thousand kinds of apples?" she asked her friends.

"You always know such weird facts," Derek commented with admiration.

"Yeah. Well, I don't believe it," said Rory. "You probably just made that one up."

"Honest," said Bolivia. "I read it somewhere."

"I doubt they'll have that many types where we're going," said Derek's mother from the front seat. "But I want to get twice as many as the last time we went picking. Apples keep for a long while, and there are so many things you can make with them."

"Did you know that eating an apple is one of the best ways to clean your teeth?" Derek's father asked.

"Sure, Dad. You tell me that every time you see me eating one," said Derek. "That's what happens when your father's a dentist," he explained to his friends.

"Then how come they don't make apple toothpaste?" Bolivia wanted to know.

Even though they'd gotten an early start, the parking lot at Hicks's Orchard was crowded. "I hope there's some left for us," grumbled Rory.

"Don't worry, kid. There's plenty for everyone," said the man who handed out cardboard carriers with handles for them to fill with apples. "The sections are labeled. The Macs are to the left and there are Rome Beauties, which are great cooking apples, on the right. There are several other types around too. You pay by weight when you're finished picking. They all cost the same. And you can eat all you want on the spot for free."

"Free? That's neat," said Derek. "I don't remember that from last time."

"Very few people ever eat more than two," the man explained. "And it's not worth policing people about eating. Just put your cores in your basket when you finish an apple. We don't want to have them all over the place.

"And if you want to pick more than one basket, bring your filled carriers here, and we'll hold them for you," the man added.

Bolivia looked around. The first time she went apple picking she had been disappointed. She had assumed that you'd climb ladders to pick the fruit. However, she had learned that most orchards cultivate dwarf trees. The apples hang low enough that ladders aren't needed at all.

"Let's start over here," said Rory, leading the way. As usual, he was making decisions for everyone.

"Pick wherever you want," said Dr. Curry.

"You can't get lost," added Derek's mother. "We'll come looking for you when we've had enough," she said as she and her husband headed toward the Rome Beauties.

"Look for apples that are perfect," Rory whispered to his friends so the other apple pickers nearby wouldn't hear him. "See. This one has a wormhole in it."

"If you ate an apple with a worm in it, you'd be cleaning your teeth and getting some protein at the same time," DeDe commented.

"Yeah. Well, you can eat worms if you want," said Rory. "I won't."

Bolivia decided that she wanted some space between herself and Rory this morning. Maybe in a little while he'd get over his sulk about DeDe's presence.

"Come on," she told DeDe. "Let's see which team will pick the most apples, the boys or the girls."

"That's no contest," said Rory. "Derek and I will beat you easy."

Bolivia didn't care who picked the most apples. But she was glad that the thought of competition was keeping Rory busy. She started picking. The air around her smelled so much like apples that before she knew it, she'd taken a bite out of one.

"Come over this way," Rory shouted to the girls as a couple of families with small children got between them.

"Why? These apples are just as good as the ones where you are," Bolivia called back, annoyed that once again Rory was trying to boss her around. And as if to prove her point, she took another bite of the apple in her hand.

Before long both Bolivia and DeDe had filled their carriers. They took them to the attendant. He labeled them and handed out empty carriers so they could continue picking.

Bolivia looked around. There were apple trees going on for about half a mile, it seemed. But off to one side there were fewer trees, and she could see a pond.

"Let's walk down there," she suggested to DeDe, pointing toward the water. It would give them a little time alone. "It's amazing about Derek's father being your dentist," she said.

"My mother always says it's a small world," said DeDe. "This proves she's right."

"It's not a small world if your parents are all the way over in Turkey," Bolivia pointed out.

"Yikes. Sorry. I forgot about that," DeDe apologized. "Do you miss them a lot?"

"Yes and no," Bolivia admitted. "They've always done a lot of traveling for their work, and I'm a pretty independent type. Sometimes I've gone with them, and other times I've stayed home. I spent a whole summer in Woodside a year ago, when they were on an archeological dig. It was great, and I couldn't wait to come back. But this time they're going to be gone six months. They're not due back until April."

"Sometimes I don't see my father for a couple of months at a time," DeDe said. "It has to do with his work schedule. But at least I always have my mother." Suddenly she broke out in a grin. "And Cookie. My dog is part of my family too. When Cookie gets into mischief, my mother says, 'I should have given your father custody of that dog,' but she's just joking."

"What kind of mischief does she get into?" asked Bolivia.

"Mostly eating. She could eat all day, like a cow," DeDe said. "We have to be so careful not to leave any food out. Not even anything that looks like food."

"What do you mean, 'looks like food'?" Bolivia asked.

"Well, we used to have a bowl of wax fruit on the coffee table in our living room. Three guesses what happened to it," DeDe said, giggling.

"Cookie ate wax fruit?" Bolivia asked.

"Yep. Did you ever hear of a dog eating wax apples, wax oranges, and wax grapes?"

"Yuck!" said Bolivia, making a face.

"You should have seen what happened when I took her for her walk. For two days she had Technicolor turds." DeDe giggled. "She was a scientific wonder."

"Oh, no." Bolivia laughed. "Didn't she get sick?"

"Nope."

"Bolivia? Where are you?" a voice called from the distance.

"That's Rory," Bolivia said. She grabbed DeDe's hand. "Come on," she said. "Let's hide from them."

The two girls ran past all the apple trees and apple pickers.

"Bolivia," Rory's voice called again. It sounded nearer than before.

"Maybe we'd better split up. It will be easier to hide that way," Bolivia said. She let go of DeDe's hand and ran toward the left, where she saw a clump of bushes. She dropped her cardboard carrier and sat down on the ground, where she was hidden by the greenery. A moment later Rory ran past, with Derek close behind.

"Bolivia?" Rory's voice called out again. He sounded really annoyed.

Bolivia snuggled under her bush and smiled at her success. Let them play hide-and-seek for a while. She'd come out when she was good and ready, not when Rory called her. She wished she could get closer to the pond, but as there were no bushes or trees there for cover, she had to stay put. She was sorry now that she was wearing shorts. The branches of the bush were scratching her arms and legs.

When she was certain that the boys had left the area, Bolivia crawled out from the bush and sat watching the ducks swimming in the pond. She knew that ducks and geese and swans all mated for life. It was one of those pieces of trivia that she

had picked up somewhere. She thought about DeDe's parents and wondered if DeDe would be upset to hear about the mating habits of those birds.

Thinking of DeDe, however, Bolivia wondered where she was hiding. She looked in every direction from where she sat. She stood up and saw Rory and Derek in the distance, walking with DeDe. She wondered if DeDe had let herself be found or if the boys had actually been successful in their search.

Now they all were probably going bananas trying to find her. Reluctantly she bent down and picked up her apple carrier.

"Where were you?" Rory demanded when Bolivia came up behind them. "We've been looking for you everywhere."

"Not everywhere," said Bolivia, smiling. "If you'd looked everywhere, you'd have found me."

"Are you bored with picking apples?" Derek asked.

"No," Bolivia told him. "I just wanted to have a look around. I watched some ducks down at the pond. I think they may be related to some other ducks I used to feed in Ithaca when I was little."

"Are you crazy?" asked Rory.

"Just crazy **about** apples," said Bolivia. She pulled an apple off the tree they were passing and took a bite. "So how many carriers have you guys filled so far?" she asked.

"Three each," said Derek proudly. "You know how many pies that means?"

"No," said Bolivia. "Do you?"

"No," Derek admitted. "But I'm ready to find out."

"I'm ready to go home," said Rory. "This isn't the way I planned for us to pick the apples."

"Tough," said Bolivia. But she said it to herself, not loud enough for Rory to hear.

Dear Mom and Dad,

I'm sitting here stuffed with apples: raw and cooked. In fact, I think my skin has turned red from all the apple eating I've done in the past few hours. Is that possible?

This morning I went apple picking with Rory and Derek and my new friend, DeDe. We picked tons of apples, and when we came home, everyone started cooking them. Derek's mother baked two apple pies at her house, and Rory's mother cooked apple-sauce in her house. Aunt Sophie made a double batch of apple cinnamon muffins here. DeDe and I went from house to house, sniffing and sampling the results, until her mother picked her up.

Before she left, I cut up one of the freshly picked apples. I let DeDe put the slices in Lucette's cage. "This house is like a zoo," DeDe said, because, of course, I also showed her the kittens.

Love from Eeny, Meeny,
Miney, Moe, Lucette, &
Bolivia

P.S. I'm beginning to feel kind of itchy all over. Could pigging out on apples do that to me?

# 5

# A Mysterious
# Disease

The discomfort that Bolivia felt Saturday evening as she wrote to her parents continued on Sunday. But it wasn't until Monday morning that she knew something was really wrong. She looked at herself in the mirror as she brushed her teeth and hardly recognized the person she saw. There were red blotches on her face, and the areas around her eyes appeared to be swollen.

She ran downstairs and called to her aunt and uncle, "What's wrong with me?"

"My heavens, you're foaming at the mouth," her aunt gasped.

Bolivia ran to the kitchen sink and spit into it. "That's just toothpaste," she said. "Look at my face."

Mr. and Mrs. Golding both examined Bolivia's face. Then they looked at each other, puzzled.

"You caught something from those dirty kittens," said her aunt. "I knew we should have gotten rid of them."

"I haven't even touched them," protested Bolivia. "They won't let me get near. You can't blame the kittens." She scratched her arm. In fact, she felt itchy all over.

"Maybe it's all those apples we ate over the weekend," her uncle suggested.

"I never got like this from eating apples before," Bolivia said. She had no idea of the number of apples she had consumed in one form or another. Still, she'd rather her aunt and uncle blamed the apples than the kittens.

"I'm going to call Dr. Curry and ask him to take a peek at you before he goes to work," Aunt Sophie said.

"Dr. Curry? He's a dentist! There's nothing wrong with my teeth," Bolivia told her aunt.

"Of course, dear. But dentists and doctors know about things like this."

"I really don't want anyone to see me," said Bolivia. She just wanted to hide in her bedroom.

"It will be all right," said her aunt, attempting to soothe Bolivia. She went to the telephone, and a few minutes later Dr. Curry was at the door.

"This isn't my specialty, you know," he said to the Goldings.

Bolivia felt herself blushing as he looked at her. But her face was already so red it probably didn't even change her appearance.

"Does anything hurt you?" Dr. Curry asked Bolivia. He put his hand to her forehead. "You don't have any fever," he announced.

"I just feel kind of itchy all over," she said. "I think I should stay home from school today."

"You're better off going to school," said Dr. Curry. "It will take your mind off it. It looks to me as if you have hives. They're an allergic reaction to something you ate. It could be one thing or a combination of foods."

"I can't go to school like this," Bolivia said. "I look like I have leprosy."

"You don't look so bad," said her uncle. Bolivia knew he was lying.

"Do you have any antihistamine?" Dr. Curry asked the Goldings. "That would reduce the swelling."

Aunt Sophie ran to the bathroom and returned with a bottle from the medicine cabinet.

Dr. Curry patted Bolivia on the shoulder before he left the Golding house. "Cheer up," he said. "You could have a toothache or need root canal work. There are all sorts of phone calls I'll be getting as soon as I arrive at my office, and they'll all be from people who would love to trade places with you."

A few minutes later Rory and Derek came to the door.

"Yikes," said Rory when he got his first look at Bolivia. "What happened to you?"

"I don't know," responded Bolivia crossly.

"My dad says she's having an allergic reaction to something," Derek reported. "You don't look so bad," he said to Bolivia.

"You're lying," said Bolivia. She turned to her aunt. "I'm *not* going to school today."

"Bolivia," said her aunt, "Dr. Curry said you could and should go. In a little while the antihistamine will start working. You'll look like your old self by the time you get there."

"No," said Bolivia. "I look gross."

"Hey, Bolivia," said Derek, "you have a pair of

sunglasses, don't you? If you wore them, you'd look okay and nobody would even know who you were."

"That's a great idea," said Uncle Lou. "You'll look like a movie star."

"Movie stars don't go to Woodside Middle School," said Bolivia. But she ran to get her sunglasses. Hiding behind them was better than nothing.

"We'd better hurry. We're going to miss the bus," said Rory, looking at his watch.

So under protest, but wearing her sunglasses, Bolivia went off to school that Monday morning.

"What's with the sunglasses?" DeDe asked on the bus.

"I really need a carton to put over my head," Bolivia responded. She slipped the glasses off for a moment so DeDe could see her face. "Pretty bad, right?"

"Not great," DeDe said. "Are you sick?"

At least she was more honest than Derek and Uncle Lou, Bolivia thought.

"I think I've developed an allergy to Woodside, New Jersey," Bolivia said. She was trying hard to treat the situation with humor, but she felt pretty miserable. Wearing sunglasses inside the bus made everything seem so dark. So in addition to feeling itchy and uncomfortable, now her vision was impaired. Still, it was a relief to be able to hide behind them.

"Bolivia, please remove those sunglasses in class," insisted Mrs. Jansen, her homeroom teacher, when she was taking attendance. Of course every head in the room turned to look at Bolivia. No one else had ever thought of wearing dark glasses in the classroom. Reluctantly Bolivia took the glasses off. At least she could see better now. But she still felt awful.

For the entire morning Bolivia sat in one class after another wishing she could hide. Maybe Dr. Curry and her aunt thought this was a good way to pass the time, but she couldn't concentrate on her German verbs or her math problems. She felt as if everyone were staring at her. And she also felt so itchy. In fact, it seemed that the only part of her body that didn't itch was her teeth. Dr. Curry would know how to explain that!

Bolivia wondered over and over what could possibly be wrong with her. She was convinced that she hadn't caught anything from the kittens. Her aunt was certainly wrong about that. But what could be the matter? Bolivia counted off on her fingers all the diseases her parents had protected themselves against before they went off on their exotic big trip: malaria, yellow fever, dengue fever, typhoid, cholera, hepatitis, schistosomiasis.

"Bolivia, by sixth grade you shouldn't need to use your fingers to do your math work," said the teacher, Mrs. Cummings.

Again everyone turned to look at Bolivia. She blushed and thought this must be absolutely the worst day of her life. If only she were thousands of miles away in Turkey with her parents. Then no one would know her name and no one would pay any attention to her.

Finally the fourth period of the morning ended, and it was time for lunch.

"Keep away from her," she overheard one girl tell another. "It could be catching." She knew they were talking about her.

"Bolivia," a voice called as she was putting some books in her locker. If her locker weren't so tiny, she would have crawled inside and closed the door.

Bolivia looked up. It was her homeroom teacher.

"Is there something wrong, dear? You don't look like your usual self today," Mrs. Jansen said.

Bolivia shrugged her shoulders.

Mrs. Jansen studied her face for a moment. "I think you should go to the nurse. Do you know where her office is?"

Bolivia nodded. It was a relief to have somewhere to go other than the lunchroom. Besides, she had absolutely no appetite. She thought of all the students eating and chattering together. They'd all be talking about her today, she realized. *The girl who turned into a hideous creature over the weekend.*

No one was in the nurse's office, but the door was open. Bolivia entered. There was a mirror on the wall, and she went over to take a look. She shuddered at her reflection. There was no question that whatever had been wrong with her when she got up this morning was much worse now. Bolivia sat on a chair while she waited. She looked at a chart on the wall that explained the major food groups, and she scratched her right leg through her jeans. Then she rolled up the denim fabric covering her leg and examined it. Her calf was covered by a red rash.

"Hello," a voice called out cheerfully. "Are you feeling ill?"

Bolivia turned toward the door. The woman standing there was wearing a pin on her shirt that identified her. She was Mrs. Arnold, the school nurse.

Bolivia licked her lips and wondered where to begin her explanation. But before she could get a word out of her mouth, the nurse spoke again.

"Young lady, you are covered with poison ivy."

"I am?" asked Bolivia incredulously. Slowly a grin covered her face. "That's wonderful."

"Wonderful? I've never in my life heard anyone call poison ivy wonderful. And from the looks of you, you have a pretty severe case of it too."

"I'd rather have poison ivy than leprosy!" exclaimed Bolivia. "My mother had poison ivy once, and she got cured."

"We'll get you cured too," the nurse promised. "You must go to a doctor after school and get a prescription. There are pills that work wonders on poison ivy these days. And in the meantime I can put some calamine lotion wherever you itch."

"Everywhere," said Bolivia simply.

"Where did you get it?" the nurse asked as she

63

began to dab Bolivia's face and arms with the cool pink liquid.

Bolivia shrugged her shoulders. She hadn't the vaguest idea where she could possibly have been exposed to the ivy leaves. There was no way Uncle Lou would let something like that grow in his yard. Then suddenly it came to her. It must have happened when she was hiding from Rory and Derek under the bush at the apple orchard. She had been so busy thinking about the boys that she hadn't even noticed the poison ivy. "I went apple picking on Saturday," she explained.

"Don't you know the difference between an apple and poison ivy?" asked the nurse.

"It's all right," said Bolivia. "I didn't eat any of the ivy."

She realized all at once that she was hungry for some lunch. She didn't care what anyone had to say about her now. She only had poison ivy. Anyone could get poison ivy. Bolivia reached into her backpack and pulled out her sunglasses.

"Would you give me a note so that I can wear these in school?" she asked the nurse.

"Of course," said Mrs. Arnold, smiling.

So Bolivia spent the rest of the day feeling itchy as she looked out from behind her dark glasses. It was a bad day, but it could have been worse. At least poison ivy was curable.

Sardis, Turkey
September 26

Dear Bolivia,

We just got your letters of September 3 and 12 today. This is a fascinating country. Our only complaint is that the mail delivery isn't as efficient as it is in the United States. We're giving this letter to one of the men who was working here and who is returning to the States tomorrow. He'll mail it when he gets home.

The dig is going well. We haven't made any *spectacular* finds, but we have made many, many small ones. And the small ones add up to a picture of civilization in the past. It's not unlike that thousand-piece jigsaw puzzle one of your friends gave you for your birthday last spring. You need patience and the conviction that you won't give up if you wish to succeed.

You asked us to write to Aunt Sophie and Uncle Lou and to tell them that you should be permitted to stay late at school. You have to remember that they've never had children, so they are going to be very protective of you until they adjust to having an eleven-and-a-half-year-old around. Here's a suggestion: Since Rory's father teaches at your school, he probably works late sometimes. Maybe you could arrange to stay late with

66

him on a particular day. Then Aunt Sophie and Uncle Lou wouldn't worry, and you'd be able to join in an extracurricular activity.

Much love to you and Aunt Sophie and Uncle Lou. Greetings to the Dunn and Curry families. And a special "hello" to Lucette. Give her some grapes and tell her they're from,

Your loving parents

# 6
# A Boy Named Aldo

"What do you mean, DeDe and a friend of hers are coming over this afternoon?" asked Rory on Thursday as they walked home from the bus stop. "We have a lot of homework to do."

Bolivia resisted the urge to scratch her face. Her aunt had taken her to the doctor, and thanks to the medicine she had prescribed, her poison ivy was much, much better.

"In the first place, I don't need your permission to invite someone over," she said. "And in the second place, why are you always so hung up about homework?" Bolivia asked, annoyed at Rory's attitude. "The homework will get done. It always does."

She realized that no matter what he said, it wasn't the homework that was bugging Rory. He didn't like Bolivia getting involved with other kids.

"They want to see the kittens," Bolivia explained to Rory and Derek. "DeDe's friend has a cat and knows a lot about animals. Maybe she'll be able to give me some advice about taking care of the kittens."

"The mother cat didn't need any advice from you or anyone else when she had the litter," Rory said.

"What do you think, Derek?" Bolivia turned to the other boy.

Derek blushed and shrugged his shoulders.

"Well, whether you like it or not, DeDe and her friend are coming in a little while. DeDe had to arrange to meet her friend and get someone to drive them over," Bolivia explained. "They're not moving in," she added, trying to placate Rory. "We'll still have time to do our homework."

But if Rory wasn't eager to entertain visitors, Mrs. Golding was just the opposite.

"Isn't it good that I baked this pan of apple gingerbread this morning?" she said when Bolivia announced that a couple of girls were coming over.

"You don't have to worry about feeding them," Bolivia said. "They just want to see the kittens. Did you look at them during the day? Did you see the mother cat? Did you feed her?"

"No, no, no, to all your questions," said Mrs. Golding.

The doorbell rang, and Bolivia ran to answer it. There stood DeDe and a familiar-looking boy.

"Hi," DeDe said. "This is my friend Aldo. He knows more about animals than any kid you'll ever meet."

Bolivia smiled at Aldo in recognition. "You're in my homeroom," she said to him. Not only was the boy in her class, but he sat right behind her because their last names were next to each other in the teacher's roll book. Bolivia Raab was followed by Aldo Sossi.

"Yeah," Aldo said. "That's right. I usually just see the back of your head, though."

"Lucky you. You missed seeing my poison ivy. The back of my head was one of the few places where I didn't have it," said Bolivia.

"I didn't know you were in the same class,"

DeDe said, laughing. "What a funny coincidence!"

"And I didn't know he was crazy about animals," Bolivia told DeDe.

"I want to be a veterinarian when I grow up," Aldo explained. "I love animals. I have two dogs and a cat at home."

"Then you'll really love these kittens," Bolivia responded. "Come on. I'll show you."

A cat whisked past them as they reached the window well. "I think that was the mother cat," Bolivia commented. "I haven't seen her near the babies, but I'm pretty sure. The coloring is similar."

"It will be almost impossible to tame her," Aldo said. "She's a real feral creature. But the kittens are still young enough that they can learn to like humans." He bent down and looked at the little creatures in the window well. "I think they're about four or five weeks old."

Aldo dug into his pockets and pulled out a pair of heavy winter gloves. "I came prepared," he said. "Do you mind if I pick one up?"

"Sure. Go right ahead if you can. They won't let me touch them," Bolivia said. She loved that Aldo had thought to ask her permission.

Aldo stepped down into the large old-fashioned window well. The kittens hissed and ran about. Bolivia and DeDe jumped back even though they were above the well. For such tiny creatures, the kittens suddenly seemed as ferocious as miniature tigers. Aldo didn't seem the least bit scared. He reached for one of them and lifted it up. The kitten hissed and squirmed, but Aldo held it firmly. Amazingly the kitten was fighting and trembling with fear at the same time.

"You've got to pet them a lot," said Aldo softly as he gently stroked the kitten in his hands. "That way they'll learn that you won't hurt them, and they'll stop being afraid. You know, if you take them to the animal shelter the way they are now, no one would want to adopt them."

"Listen," whispered Bolivia, leaning close to Aldo and the kitten. "He's purring." She put her hand out to touch the kitten. Immediately it turned its attention to her and hissed, showing its small, sharply pointed teeth. Bolivia quickly backed away. She noticed how the kitten was clinging to Aldo's gloves. Tiny claws were extended from each paw. No wonder Aldo was wearing gloves and a thick jacket.

"It's too bad there are so many of them," DeDe said. "If there was just one or two, it would be a lot easier to tame them. It's going to be an awful big job to tame four individual little wildcats."

"It's hard, but it can be done," said Aldo, continuing to pet the kitten he was holding. "Besides, you're lucky that they're in this window well. If they were out on ground level, you'd never be able to catch them. Here they're trapped—at least until they get bigger. Unless the mother carries them out, they're stuck where they are. And I bet they're too big by now for her to do that."

Aldo put down the kitten he was holding and reached for another. "The mother cat is waiting for them to get out on their own. It'll show her they're big enough to take care of themselves."

"So it's like they're in a cage," DeDe observed.

"Right," said Aldo.

"Wait a minute. I'll be right back," said Bolivia. "I want to get a pair of gloves too."

She rushed into the house and hurried up the stairs. It was lucky she had unpacked everything so recently that she knew just where to look for her thick winter gloves.

When she returned to the window well, Bolivia

saw Rory and Derek approaching. "Hi," she called to them. "I'm glad you came over." She turned to Aldo. "These are my friends Rory Dunn and Derek Curry. They live on either side of this house."

"Hi," Aldo said. "I'm showing Bolivia how to make the kittens less afraid of humans. If you had gloves on, I'd let you take this kitten for a bit. But you'll get really scratched up the way you are."

Derek nodded his head by way of greeting, but Rory stood scowling at this new boy. He must have thought that DeDe's friend would be a girl, Bolivia thought. Just as she had.

Suddenly Aldo looked up and said, "Hey, Rory, are you related to the Mr. Dunn who teaches English at our school?"

"Yeah," said Rory. "He's my dad. Are you in his class?"

"No," said Aldo, shaking his head. "But my sister, Karen, had him in eighth grade. Your dad was wonderful. He let her write all her reports on her pink stationery with little flowers along the border because she used to panic when she saw a sheet of loose-leaf paper. Karen got the first A of her life in your dad's class, and it kind of turned her around.

She doesn't hate school anymore." Aldo paused. "He's a neat teacher. I hope I get him before I finish middle school."

"Gee," said Bolivia, "I like your father, Rory, but I never knew that about him. Now I like him even more."

"I hope I get him too," said DeDe.

"Yeah. He's okay," said Rory. Bolivia could see that even though he was trying to act cool, he couldn't help being pleased with the praise for his father.

"That's really funny," DeDe observed. "First it turned out that Derek's father is my dentist, and now this coincidence. It *is* a small world."

Bolivia turned to Rory. "Would you like to borrow my gloves?" she asked him. "Aldo says if the kittens are handled a bit every day, then they'll become tame. If we all take turns, we can do it."

"I don't care," Rory said, shrugging his shoulders, but he reached out for Bolivia's winter gloves all the same.

Aldo put down the kitten he had been holding and offered his gloves to Derek. Eventually each of the five kids had a chance to hold one of the kittens.

"By the way," Aldo said, "there's going to be a special nature film on TV tonight about all types of cats. I heard them announce it a couple of days ago."

"Bolivia doesn't watch television," Rory said. "It's against her principles."

"What do you mean?" Aldo asked, puzzled.

"Well, I mostly think people watch too much TV. So I don't watch. But I'll be sure to look at that program tonight. I need to find out all I can about cats if I have four of them right here."

Bolivia remembered a saying that she'd seen on a T-shirt: A stranger is a friend you haven't yet gotten to know.

Aldo and DeDe were no longer strangers. They were new friends for her. They could be new friends for Rory and Derek too, if they gave them a chance.

October 5

Dear Mom and Dad,

A boy from school came and showed me how to tame the kittens. If Rory, Derek, and I play with them every day, they will become used to people. I've petted them all, but I'm falling in love with Moe. Would you let me adopt him?

Love,
Bolivia

## POSTCARD

Arlene & Gerald Raab
Cornell U. Excavations
Site #2
Sardis, Turkey

# 7
# A Rain Forest in Bolivia

No outing had been planned for Saturday. Rory, Derek, and Bolivia were supposed to be helping rake up and bag leaves for Mr. Golding. Mostly they were jumping into the piles of leaves and laughing together.

Mrs. Golding called out the window, "Bolivia, your friend DeDe is on the phone!"

Bolivia shook the leaves off her clothing and ran into the house. "Hi," she said to DeDe. "What's up?"

"Would it be okay for Aldo and me to come by again to see the kittens?" DeDe asked. "I just told him about your parrot, and he's crazy for a chance to see her too."

"Sure," agreed Bolivia eagerly. "Come on over."

"We're on our way," said DeDe, and the phone line went dead.

Bolivia thought Rory and Derek would be pleased to see Aldo and DeDe. Unfortunately Rory was in one of his difficult moods. "Why do they have to come over again?" he complained when Bolivia announced that they would be joined shortly by her new friends.

"Why not?" replied Bolivia. She grabbed an armload of leaves and stuffed them into a large plastic bag. She really felt like stuffing Rory into the bag. Who needed him when he acted so disagreeably?

"Where is she? Where is she?" Aldo asked twenty minutes later, when his father dropped him and DeDe off at the Goldings' house.

"I told you he was excited about your parrot," DeDe said to Bolivia.

"Bolivia's parrot can say my name and Derek's," Rory said, scowling at the two visitors.

"But she doesn't do it very often," Derek admitted.

"I don't care what she says. I just want a chance to see her," said Aldo.

Bolivia smiled at him. She was impressed by his

79

interest in animals and the fact that he knew that he wanted to be a veterinarian when he grew up. She had absolutely no idea about what she wanted to do in the future. It seemed too far away to even think about.

"Don't you want to see the kittens this morning?" Bolivia asked. "Lucette won't fly away."

They walked around to the side of the house. The four kittens were sleeping huddled together.

"I keep watching for the mother cat, but I hardly ever see her," Bolivia told Aldo.

"She must be getting ready to wean the kittens," said Aldo. "I can see that they've grown just since we last saw them. Besides," he added, "I bet she hates the way they smell now too."

"What do you mean, the way they smell?" Bolivia asked him.

"They pick up the scent of all the humans who have been handling them. Wild animals don't like the smell of humans," Aldo explained.

Rory leaned close to Aldo and inhaled. "You're right," he said. "You do stink."

Bolivia turned toward Rory. She could not believe how rude and mean he was acting.

Luckily Aldo just laughed. "Animals are super-sensitive to smells. And to a feral cat I would have a very bad odor," he said. "And so would you," he added, looking at Rory.

Bolivia smiled. She was glad that Aldo could give it back to Rory.

"Let's go look at Lucette," DeDe said, changing the subject. Bolivia smiled at her friend gratefully as they all trooped up the stairs of the Golding house and crowded into her bedroom.

"She's beautiful!" Aldo exclaimed as soon as he saw the parrot. It was the one thing he could say that Rory wouldn't argue about. He admired the bird too.

"Good morning. Have a nice day," squawked the parrot.

"It's a pleasure to meet you," Aldo told the bird. He stuck a finger through the cage and gently stroked Lucette's green feathers. Lucette began to show off by climbing with her strong claws up the bars of the cage. Then, satisfied that she had impressed them all, she returned to her previous activity, which was eating kernels off an ear of uncooked corn.

"She'd be fantastic in our rain forest," Aldo told Bolivia.

"What rain forest?" Bolivia wanted to know.

"I belong to the afterschool nature club. We've been studying rain forests in different countries. And we're also making a rain forest in an empty classroom."

"How can you *make* a rain forest?" demanded Derek. "That's something that happens in nature. We learned all about it back in fourth grade."

"Well, it's a *simulation* of a rain forest. You'll have to come and see it," Aldo said. "We've painted backdrops of trees and plants. And then we added some big rubber plants that a couple of parents let us borrow. And we've put carpet padding down on the floor and covered it with dirt."

"Dirt? You brought dirt into school?" asked Rory incredulously. "I wonder if my father knows about that."

"Yeah. We got a special deal from one of the garden centers. We bought a couple of fifty-pound sacks of dirt and spread it all over the floor. Someone had a humidifier that he let us use, so it makes the room very damp. And we have an electric heater to make the room hotter than the rest of the school. We've borrowed some stuffed toy animals from kids who have little brothers and sisters."

"I've seen them," said DeDe. "There are three monkeys in different sizes climbing up the rubber plants. It's like a Curious George family reunion."

"We took off their clothes," Aldo pointed out. "They were all wearing little red shirts and caps. Spider monkeys in the rain forest wouldn't have that."

"Naked monkeys?" said Rory, pretending to be shocked. "What will you think of next? A nudist colony in the rain forest?"

"Don't forget the snakes," DeDe told Aldo.

"Snakes?" Bolivia asked.

"At first we planned to use rubber snakes, but one of the guys in the club has a couple of pet snakes. He's going to bring them in one afternoon. And if we could borrow Lucette, well, that would be just perfect," said Aldo enthusiastically.

"I don't think you should take Lucette to school," said Rory.

"Don't they have tropical rain forests where she comes from?" asked DeDe, ignoring Rory's comment.

"Yeah. I'm pretty sure they do," Aldo said. "We

have a map with all the rain forests in the world marked on it."

"Well, if Bolivia comes to the nature club, you'll have Bolivia in a rain forest instead of a rain forest in Bolivia," said DeDe, delighted by this possibility.

"I'll definitely come," Bolivia promised. "But I'll have to think about bringing Lucette. It might be too much for her," she said.

"I'm sure it would be too much for her," said Rory. "Too many people, too much noise. You'd better keep her home," he told Bolivia.

Bolivia looked at Rory. He didn't know it, but he had just helped her make up her mind. Of course she would take Lucette to the rain forest. The parrot would probably feel right at home there even if it weren't the real thing. It sounded like a lot of fun, and the way Rory was acting these days, anything he opposed was beginning to sound great to Bolivia.

"The music teacher found us a tape with sounds of the rain forest. It has a lot of birds and insect noises on it," Aldo mentioned.

"It's really neat," said DeDe.

"I didn't know you were in the nature club too," Bolivia said.

"I'm not. It meets at the same time as the school band, and I can't be in two places at once. But sometimes I run into the rain forest to take a peek before I go to the music room. You have to see it to believe it. It's really cool."

"With an electric heater, it sounds *hot*," said Rory.

"When do you meet?" Bolivia asked Aldo.

"Tuesday afternoons," he reported.

"Let's all go this coming Tuesday," Bolivia suggested to Rory and Derek.

Derek looked at Rory, who shrugged. Bolivia could see that Rory was curious about the idea of a rain forest right inside the school building. But as usual, since it wasn't his idea, he wasn't going to admit his interest to her.

Bolivia didn't care. She'd go to the rain forest with or without Rory and Derek. She just hoped it would work out with Rory's father's schedule, the way her parents had suggested. But if it didn't, she'd still arrange somehow to stay after school. Maybe just this once Uncle Lou could pick her up.

"We even eat rain forest snacks," Aldo suddenly remembered to say.

"What kind of snacks?" asked Derek with interest.

"Nuts. Fruits. We had pineapple last week and cashew nuts. It's all good," said Aldo. "You'd like it."

"You're making me hungry," DeDe complained. "It's bad enough watching Lucette eating her lunch."

"I could find another raw ear of corn if you really want it," Bolivia teased.

"No, thanks. Aldo and I are going out to have pizza. Why don't you all come along?"

Bolivia didn't wait for Rory and Derek to respond. "Sure," she said. "We all love pizza. We once even had a contest to see who could eat the most."

"Who won?" Aldo asked.

"It was a tie," Bolivia said. "A three-way tie."

"So long, Lucette," DeDe called to the parrot.

"Have a nice day." Lucette didn't look up from her corncob, but she squawked out her message. "Have a nice day," she repeated as the five middle school students left the room.

"I don't like onions or mushrooms on my pizza," said Rory. "And neither does Derek."

And that was how Bolivia knew the two boys would be joining her and Aldo and DeDe for lunch.

"I do," said Aldo. "But I also love extra cheese. That's the greatest."

"That's my favorite," Derek said. "And Rory's too."

"Stop talking about food until we get there," Rory said. "I'm starving."

Bolivia grinned. She was suddenly feeling very hopeful that with the assistance of Aldo and DeDe she was going to do the impossible. She was going to help Rory and Derek make some new friends and get some new ideas. Maybe they'd even try mushrooms on their pizza one of these days.

Dear Mom and Dad,

Did you get my card asking whether I can keep Moe? I hope you say yes. He's such a darling. I know you'll love him. In the meantime, though, I realized that I had to convince Aunt Sophie and Uncle Lou that it was a good idea to have a kitten around the house too. It won't do me any good if you both agree and they say no. I don't want to leave Moe outdoors all winter long. He could freeze to death!

My problem is that Aunt Sophie keeps saying that kittens are dirty and if we had one, it would make a mess.

Tonight a little field mouse got into the house and ran across the kitchen floor while she was fixing supper. Aunt Sophie ran squealing into the living room. When she calmed down, Uncle Lou said, "I guess if there was a kitten in the house, you wouldn't have to worry about mice." I almost ran across the room and gave him a hug. But then Aunt Sophie shook her head no. "Tomorrow we'll buy a mousetrap," she said. How will I ever get her to agree to my keeping Moe?

Love and hugs,
Bolivia

# 8
# Bolivia in a Rain Forest

On Monday, as soon as they finished eating their lunches, Aldo took Bolivia to peek inside the room that the nature club had transformed into its rain forest. Even though neither the humidifier nor the heater was turned on when she arrived, Bolivia could still feel the dampness and smell the earthy odor in the air. There was a soft cushion of soil underfoot as she walked inside the room.

Mr. Peters, the adviser to the club, was there, busily watering the rubber plants.

"Hello," he said to them. "Have you come to investigate another corner of the world?"

"This is a girl from my homeroom named

Bolivia Raab," said Aldo, introducing his classmate to the teacher. "She's got a real live parrot at home. I asked her to bring it to our club tomorrow."

"A parrot? That's fantastic!" exclaimed Mr. Peters. "What type is it?"

"She's a green Amazon parrot from South America," Bolivia explained. "I've had her since I was very young, and I've taught her to speak a little."

"Wonderful!" said Mr. Peters enthusiastically. "I bet she'd feel right at home here in our rain forest. Will you bring her to school tomorrow?"

Bolivia really was intrigued by the idea of Lucette visiting the rain forest. It seemed only fair that the bird should be given the experience. She had lived for so many years away from the tropical environment that was a parrot's natural habitat. Nevertheless, Bolivia worried that a whole day at school was more than Lucette needed. It was stressful enough for a student. Imagine how it would be for a bird!

Bolivia thought about all the students who would try to touch Lucette during the day when she wasn't around to protect her. There was bound to be some wise guy who would poke the parrot and possibly hurt her.

Mr. Peters seemed to guess what she was thinking. "We'd be very careful that no harm comes to your bird," he reassured her.

"Let me see if my uncle can drive her over to school in the afternoon in time for your club meeting," Bolivia offered. That seemed the perfect compromise. An hour and a half in the afternoon should be enough rain forest adventure for Lucette.

"Wonderful!" Mr. Peters exclaimed again. "I'll tell Kenny to bring his snakes to school tomorrow too. And I'll announce over the public address system that the rain forest will be open to the entire school."

Bolivia knew that most of the time no one paid any attention to the announcements. Otherwise she would have been worried about a thousand students trying to squeeze into the rain forest.

"Neat," said Aldo as a bell interrupted the conversation. He turned to Bolivia. "We'd better go," he said. "Our lunch period is over."

"Okay," Bolivia said. "See you tomorrow," she called to the science teacher.

Mr. Golding was perfectly willing to deliver Lucette to the middle school the next day. "It's been a long time since I was inside a school," he commented. "Do you think they'll let me take some pictures of that rain forest?"

"Why not?" asked Bolivia. "I bet they'll be thrilled. And then I could send a picture to my parents too."

The next afternoon, just at the time when school was being dismissed, Bolivia's uncle Lou arrived there with Lucette. It was a day as warm as summer, so Bolivia hadn't worried about the outdoor temperature being too cold for her parrot. But her uncle was the cautious type. He had Lucette's traveling cage wrapped in a big blanket when he met Bolivia in the school lobby.

Rory and Derek were waiting with Bolivia.

"Poor Lucette," Rory said. "Having to go to school at her age."

"What is her age?" asked Derek.

"She's older than we are," Bolivia responded. "She's about twenty years old."

"What's in there?" asked a boy passing by in the hall. In a moment they were surrounded by a group of students curious about the large bundle in Mr. Golding's arms.

"Stand back. Stand back," Bolivia shouted. "This is my parrot, Lucette, and she's going to make a visit to the rain forest upstairs. If you want to see her, you'll have to wait on line outside the science room. Too many people at once will scare her."

Luckily at that very moment Mr. Peters joined them, and he too announced to the students that the only way to see the parrot was to visit the rain forest.

Then Bolivia, Rory, Derek, Mr. Golding (holding the parrot in the wrapped cage), and Mr. Peters (holding back the crowd) made their way up the flight of stairs and toward the room that housed the rain forest. Outside the doorway of the forest stood Aldo, DeDe, and several other students Bolivia didn't know.

Mr. Peters unlocked the door, and they all went

inside. The science teacher turned on both the humidifier and the electric heater.

"This is amazing," gasped Mr. Golding, marveling at the room's decor. "Look at that." He pointed to some pieces of rope that had been painted green and hung from the ceiling. "They look just like wild vines."

"It even smells like a rain forest, doesn't it?" Bolivia asked her uncle.

"How do you know?" asked Rory. "Have you ever been in a real rain forest?"

"No. But I've been in hothouses in botanical gardens where they grow tropical plants. They always smell just like this room."

"Let me get my snakes," said one of the boys who was standing nearby. "They've been waiting in here all day." He went over to a cardboard box that had holes punched in it and removed the lid.

Mr. Golding put Lucette's cage down on the floor and removed the blanket. Everyone gathered around to stare at the parrot.

"Tell them my name," Rory demanded of the bird. "Say Rory. Go on. Rory. Say Rory," he repeated.

The parrot blinked her black eyes but didn't say a word.

Bolivia bent down and opened the cage. She carefully removed Lucette and let the parrot stand on her arm.

"I could put her on one of the rubber plants," she offered to Mr. Peters.

"Hello there. Happy New Year," Lucette suddenly squawked. Apparently she now felt ready to show off.

"There are so many people here she probably thinks it's a party," Bolivia said, laughing. She rubbed her hand across her face. It was warm in the rain forest, and her face was damp with sweat.

"Happy New Year to you," DeDe called out. "I've got to go," she told Bolivia. "They're expecting me at the band rehearsal. I'll call you tonight to find out how Lucette liked the rain forest."

"So long," Aldo said to DeDe.

"Who's in charge of the sound effects?" asked Mr. Peters.

"It's my turn," one of the girls told him. She went over to a corner where there was a cassette player half-hidden behind a rubber plant. She turned on a switch, and at once the room was filled with tropical noises. There was the sound of dripping water. And there were many birdcalls. In fact, it seemed as if the room was filled with tropical birds.

"Hello there," squawked Lucette.

"She must think she's listening to real birds," said Derek.

"Watch out," warned Kenny, the owner of the two grass snakes. "You almost stepped on Jefferson."

Bolivia looked down. There was a green snake moving in front of her just as if she were walking in a real rain forest.

Mr. Golding took the blanket and the birdcage and placed them in the hallway outside the room. They didn't belong inside a rain forest. Then he took his camera out of the case around his neck and began to take pictures of one of the more realistic toy monkeys climbing on a plant. "I wish people could smell these pictures when they're developed," he told the science teacher. "You've done a fantastic job here."

Bolivia noticed Rory turning the dial on the electric heater. She hoped he was lowering the heat. She was really feeling uncomfortably warm.

"Hello. Can I come in or do I need a passport?" a woman's voice called out at the doorway.

Bolivia turned to see who had entered the room. It was Dr. Osborne, the assistant principal of the school.

"Come in. Come in," called Mr. Peters. "We have everything here except mosquitoes."

"This is lovely. Just lovely," Dr. Osborne told the teacher.

"The nature club has done a lot of hard work to create all this," Mr. Peters informed her proudly.

"Happy New Year!" Lucette squawked from her perch on a rubber plant.

"Happy New Year?" Dr. Osborne walked toward the corner where Bolivia and Lucette were stationed.

"Watch your step!" shouted Kenny as the assistant principal narrowly missed trampling on one of his snakes.

Dr. Osborne looked down and gave an amazingly loud shriek. It was much louder than the one that Bolivia's aunt Sophie had given when she'd seen the mouse in the kitchen.

At that moment Bolivia felt a few drops of rain

on her face. Then it started raining harder. She looked up at the ceiling. How in the world had Mr. Peters and his students arranged that?

Some of the students in the room began to rush out the door, but others remained, lifting their faces toward the water and enjoying the unexpected shower.

"It's just a little grass snake. He won't hurt you," said Kenny, but the assistant principal was already out the door. Bolivia wondered if she was looking to get out of the rain or to put more distance between herself and Kenny's snake.

"Get the blanket," she shouted to her uncle. The cool water felt good on her skin, but she thought she'd better protect Lucette.

"Where's this water coming from?" Aldo asked Mr. Peters. Apparently he was just as surprised as Bolivia by the rain.

"It's the sprinkler system," Mr. Peters answered. "The heat in the room seems to have triggered it." He had unplugged the electric heater. Now he was busily opening the windows, which were hidden behind painted backdrops.

"I never heard of having windows in a rain forest," Rory said. His eyeglasses were spattered with water drops, and his hair looked as if he'd been interrupted in the middle of a shower.

"Go and get the custodian," Mr. Peters instructed Aldo. "He'll know how to shut off the sprinklers."

Dr. Osborne returned to the classroom, holding an umbrella over her head. "Where's that snake?" she asked nervously.

"Here," called out Kenny, holding up his grass snake. "This is Jefferson. You scared him."

"I scared him? He scared *me*," the assistant principal said.

"Then you'd better watch out for Washington, my other snake. He's hiding under one of the plants."

"You mean, there are *two* snakes in this room? Snakes are not in my job description." Dr. Osborne looked anxiously down toward her feet.

"Happy New Year, RoryDerek!" squawked Lucette from under the blanket that Bolivia had thrown over her. This was very unusual. Generally Lucette was silent when she was covered up.

The entrance to the science room was jammed with students and teachers from the other clubs that had been meeting along the corridor. Every-

one was curious about the screams and the water puddles that had oozed out of the science room.

The custodian arrived, shaking his head in dismay. "First it was dirt," he mumbled. "Now this." He carried a ladder, which he climbed on to reach a switch near the ceiling. The rain stopped as suddenly as it had begun, but the air was more humid than ever. Just the way the air should be in a rain forest, Bolivia realized as she pulled at her wet T-shirt. She looked down at her jeans, which were spattered with mud.

Dr. Osborne closed her umbrella. Mr. Peters smiled at her. "This is how we keep education alive and exciting," he explained. "These students will always remember about rain forests now."

"You can say that again," said the assistant principal. "I'll never forget this afternoon or the snakes."

"Jefferson is harmless," Kenny reassured her. "And so is Washington. Nothing bad could have happened to you." He broke into a grin. "But I am saving up for a boa constrictor."

"If you get one, don't ever bring it to school," Dr. Osborne said firmly.

"They don't eat people. Just mice," Kenny said.

The assistant principal turned to the science teacher. "This was a wonderful display," she said. "I'm sure everyone has learned a great deal from this. But perhaps it's time for you to move on to another area of study."

"Good idea," said the custodian. "I can't wait to get the dirt out of this school."

"Oh, I have plenty of other plans," Mr. Peters told Dr. Osborne. "I thought we'd turn this room into a moonscape. There are no snakes on the moon," he added.

"You never told me school was so exciting," commented Bolivia's uncle Lou as he drove the three damp and dirty kids and the parrot back home at the end of the afternoon. "I think I wouldn't mind being eleven years old all over again."

"This was special," said Bolivia. "I wouldn't call it a typical day."

"Neither would I," said Derek.

"Besides, if you came back to school, you'd have two pages of math homework to do tonight," Rory pointed out.

"In that case I guess I'm glad I'm not eleven. I

don't want to do homework. I'm going to develop my pictures tonight. I think I got some beauties."

"Happy New Year," Lucette said from the backseat.

Dear Mom and Dad,

This is what's happening here:

1. Lucette spent an afternoon in an imitation rain forest at school. The next day the forest was destroyed (sort of like what's happening out in the real world), and now there's an imitation surface of the moon in its place.

2. Aldo says the kittens are just about old enough and tame enough to be adopted. Rory's mother has agreed that the Dunn family can take one. And a couple of families down our street have expressed interest too. But Aunt Sophie still refuses. So I have to decide whether to let someone else take Moe or try to keep him inside the window well a bit longer in case I can get her to change her mind.

3. Uncle Lou keeps taking pictures like they were giving film away for free. I decided that instead of sending you individual pictures, I'm going to make a little album of everything that happens here. At the rate I'm going, the album is half-filled already, and I've been here only a month and a half!

4. I started going to the afterschool choral group. It's great. I really look forward to it. Rory's father brings me home when it's over.

5. Rory and Derek are acting real weird sometimes. I wonder if it has to do with hormones. Dad, were you difficult when you were eleven and a half?

Love & hugs,
Bolivia

# 9
# Eeny, Meeny, Miney, Moe

Experience had taught Bolivia that a friendship with Rory Dunn was full of ups and downs. One minute he was laughing and full of good ideas, and the next minute he was annoyed because he wasn't getting his own way. He got along fine with Derek because Derek always gave in. Bolivia was willing to give in sometimes too. But she wasn't always going to agree with him just for the sake of their friendship. What kind of friendship was it if one person set all the terms?

"Why do you invite those kids, Aldo and DeDe, over every day?" Rory complained to Bolivia. The two of them were walking home from school with Derek a few days after their visit to the rain forest.

Bolivia had been sitting next to DeDe on the bus, and that always annoyed Rory.

"They don't come every day. *You* come every day," Bolivia retorted. "Aldo and DeDe were here only twice. Why don't you like them?"

"Who needs them?" was Rory's answer.

And Bolivia realized once again that even worse than the bossiness that was part of Rory's personality was the fact that he became jealous so easily. He resented the fact that she wanted more friends than just Derek and himself.

Bolivia decided to ignore him when he acted that way. And so she shrugged and said, "Eeny, Meeny, Miney, and Moe needed them for sure. Look how Aldo taught us how to tame the kittens. Aldo says that if they weren't tamed, no one would want to adopt them. They'd either become feral cats like their mother or be put to sleep by the animal shelter."

She shuddered at the thought of the kittens being killed. Nowadays they were so accustomed to her that instead of resisting or hiding in a corner, they raced across the bottom of the well to greet her. Moe even tried to climb up the leg of her jeans. And she no longer needed gloves to handle them.

"Too bad your aunt won't let you adopt one," Derek said.

"Do you think you could take Moe for me?" Bolivia asked him. "Just till I go back to Ithaca?"

"I can't," Derek said. "I'm afraid he'll attack Hamlet. Hamsters can't help it if they resemble mice. And even though Hamlet is supposed to stay in his cage, he escapes at least a couple of times a week."

Bolivia nodded. She had thought of that herself. A cold wind started blowing, and Bolivia pulled up the hood of her sweatshirt. It was hard to believe that just a couple of days ago the weather had been so warm.

"What about you?" Bolivia asked Rory. "Could you take Moe for me? Temporarily," she added. She wanted to be sure she'd get Moe back when it was time to return to Ithaca.

Rory looked doubtful. "I had a really hard time convincing my mother that we should adopt one. She's afraid Edna will be too rough with the kitten and get scratched or something." He thought for a moment. "Maybe I can get her to agree on a second kitten," he said. "It would be too bad if you couldn't keep Moe."

"Thanks," said Bolivia gratefully. Sometimes Rory could be very sweet.

The three friends reached Dogleg Lane and walked immediately to the side of the Golding house. "Hi, babies. Here I am," Bolivia called out as she dropped her backpack and crouched down by the window well.

Usually the cats slept together in one big mass of fur. They would wake when Bolivia and the boys arrived. This afternoon, however, it was quiet in the window well. There were some dried leaves that had fallen into the well from the nearby trees but no kittens in any of the four corners. Bolivia stood frozen to the spot.

"Where can they be?" she asked Rory and Derek. Her voice cracked with emotion. Of course they had no better idea than Bolivia did.

"Aunt Sophie? Uncle Lou?" she called, running into the house. "The kittens are gone!"

"I saw them just a little while ago," Bolivia's uncle said. "I had a couple of shots left on my roll of film, so I went outside and photographed them to finish it up. That was just after lunch," he added.

"That's ages ago," said Bolivia. So much could have happened to the kittens since then.

"Maybe the mother cat removed them from the window well," suggested Aunt Sophie.

"Maybe they climbed out on their own," said Derek. He and Rory had followed Bolivia.

"We've got to hunt for them," Bolivia said. "And we have to hurry. Look how dark it's getting already. Maybe I should call Aldo. He knows so much about animals. He might have a good idea about how to find them."

"Aldo doesn't know everything," grumbled Rory. "If the kittens are around, we'll find them."

"I think those are rain clouds overhead," Aunt Sophie said.

So Bolivia, Rory, and Derek began looking everywhere. Rory stopped to tell his mother about the missing kittens, and she and Edna joined the search party. Uncle Lou also came along.

"There are so many bushes and so many leaves they could be hiding under," said Rory as their feet crunched on the fallen autumn leaves.

"They could have gone off this block," Derek mentioned.

"And they may have gone off in different directions," Bolivia added. Would Moe choose north, south, east, or west? She shivered as a gust of wind blew some of the leaves into the air. "They're so little," she said. "And they'll be hungry too." Then she had another thought. "If they went out onto the street, they could get hit by a car."

"They're stray cats, after all," Uncle Lou pointed out. "They know instinctively how to take care of themselves. That's how stray cats survive."

"They don't all make it," Bolivia said, choking back a sob.

"Here, kitty, kitty, kitty," she heard Edna calling from her yard.

"I just felt a drop of rain," Rory called out.

"Oh, no," moaned Bolivia as she too felt a few cold drops on her face. This was the real thing. Not like the drops from the school sprinkler system.

"We'd better go in," said Uncle Lou. "Otherwise we'll get soaked."

"The kittens will get soaked wherever they are," said Bolivia. "We've got to keep looking."

"Maybe they've hidden in someone's garage or under a car or something," said Derek hopefully.

"Bolivia. Lou," called Aunt Sophie, coming from the house. She was holding a large umbrella. "You'd better come inside now," she said. "I don't want either of you catching a cold. Or you boys either," she added, looking at Rory and Derek.

"But they need me," Bolivia protested. "The kittens need me." She sniffed back some tears. "Poor Moe," she said, remembering the last time she had held his tiny body and felt him purring.

"They have a mother somewhere," said her uncle, taking her by the arm. "She'll find them and take care of them. She's probably with them right now."

"I knew I should have called Aldo," said Bolivia as she went reluctantly with her uncle.

Of course, Bolivia had no appetite for supper. She kept thinking about the kittens as she listened to the rain coming down outside. Were they drenched? Were they huddling together for

warmth? Or had they gotten separated from one another?

It was with great difficulty that Bolivia tackled her German homework. She had to read a chapter in her social studies book too. Her eyes looked at the words, but she couldn't concentrate. Her mind was on the kittens all the time.

Finally it was time to get ready for bed. "Have a nice day," Lucette squawked as Bolivia covered her cage.

"How can I have a nice day or a nice night when I'm worrying about those poor tiny, wet, frozen kittens?" Bolivia complained to her parrot.

Aunt Sophie knocked on the door and then came inside. "Bolivia," she said, "why don't you let me bring you a glass of milk and a couple of cookies? You hardly had any supper at all."

"Thanks," said Bolivia, hugging her aunt. "But I'm not hungry. I keep worrying about the kittens."

"I'm sure they're fine," said her aunt. "Didn't that boy, Aldo, explain to you about feral cats and how they are able to take care of themselves?"

"I know. But these aren't feral anymore. They've been tamed. They're used to being fed.

They've never hunted for their own food or taken care of themselves," said Bolivia, wiping a tear that was sliding down her cheek.

"Oh, honey," said Aunt Sophie, "there's nothing we can do tonight. So try to get some sleep. We'll look for them some more tomorrow. I shouldn't even tell you this now, but I was beginning to weaken about letting you adopt that little kitten. You know, the one you wanted, that you called Moe. So here's what we'll do. If the kittens don't turn up, we can go to the animal shelter and you can pick out another kitten for yourself. How about that?" she asked her niece.

"Oh, Aunt Sophie, that's so sweet of you," said Bolivia, no longer able to keep back the tears. "But I don't want another one. I want Moe." She reached for a tissue and blew her nose. Then she kissed her aunt.

"Your uncle is going to develop his pictures. He told me he was planning to blow up the best one and put it in a frame for you," Aunt Sophie said. "I'll bet you'll like that."

"Thanks," said Bolivia. She got under the covers, and her aunt turned off the light for her. She knew her aunt and uncle meant well. A picture of

116

the kittens would be nice. But what good was that? It was bad enough that she had a framed picture of her parents sitting on the chest of drawers. Now Eeny, Meeny, Miney, and Moe would be reduced to an image on paper, cold to the touch.

Dear Mom and Dad,

Something wonderful happened and something terrible. Luckily the terrible thing was first, so there is a happy ending. This is the terrible thing. Eeny, Meeny, Miney, and Moe disappeared. The window well was empty when I came home from school yesterday. We all looked everywhere, but we couldn't find the kittens.

Before I went to bed, Aunt Sophie said she was going to let me adopt Moe after all. The only problem was, there was no Moe.

Well, guess what? This morning all four kittens were waiting back inside the well. We decided that they are able to get in and out of the well on their own, but they returned because they consider it their *home*.

Of course, I scooped up Moe and took him right inside the house. There was no way I wanted to risk his going traveling again and perhaps getting hit by a car or lost. Rory picked up Eeny (but it's possible he'll give her a new name) and took her inside his house. It was hard to go to school after that, but Aunt Sophie insisted.

While I was gone, she and Uncle Lou took Moe to a vet. They wanted to check that he was in good health and didn't have fleas. Guess what? He did. Also ear mites.

The vet sprayed him with a special powder and promised that the fleas and mites will soon be gone. I bet if he hadn't been almost lost, Aunt Sophie would never have agreed to let him stay inside until she was 100 percent sure the fleas were gone.

The two remaining kittens are being adopted by some people down the street. And the mother cat seems to have gone away. It's a little sad that the kittens will never see their mother again. But I guess that's the way it is with animals. I'm glad it's not like that with people!

Moe is sleeping on my lap right now. He purrs so loudly you could almost hear him all the way in Turkey, if you listen hard. (Just joking.) But you'll hear him when you come home.

Love from Aunt Sophie, Uncle Lou, Lucette, Moe, and me too.

> Your very happy
> daughter,
> Bolivia

# 10
# The Ups & Downs
# of Friendship

Octtober 31 fell on a Friday. A week and a half before, DeDe phoned Bolivia and invited her to a Halloween party and supper to be held after school. She also asked for Rory's and Derek's phone numbers so she could invite them as well.

Bolivia got off the phone and told her aunt and uncle about the invitation. "What will you wear as a costume?" her aunt asked.

"I don't know," said Bolivia. "Maybe Rory and Derek and I can think of something to do together," she said. That idea really appealed to her.

"Like the Three Musketeers," suggested Uncle Lou. He was sitting with both the newspaper and Moe in his lap.

"Or the Three Little Pigs." Bolivia giggled.

"There's the Three Bears too, but I don't think Rory would like that. He's the shortest, so he'd have to go as the baby bear. He'd hate that." Bolivia knew Rory was sensitive about his height.

Twenty minutes later the phone rang. It was DeDe again. "Do I have bad breath?" she asked Bolivia.

"No. What kind of question is that?" Bolivia wanted to know.

"I'm just trying to figure out why Rory was so quick to turn down the invitation to my party. He didn't even give any excuse about why he couldn't come."

"Maybe he's going somewhere with his parents that day or something," suggested Bolivia. She said that to make DeDe feel better. Secretly she was pretty sure this was just another example of Rory's off again, on again antisocial behavior.

"I don't know," said DeDe. "He just said that he wouldn't come. And then when I called Derek, he said the same thing. He tried to make up some sort of excuse, but it was so phony that I could see through it like a window."

"Well, forget it," said Bolivia. "I'm coming, and whoever else you ask will probably come too. Rory and Derek always stick together, and they do things and don't do things as a team. It's their problem if they don't want to come."

"You're sure it isn't me?" asked DeDe. "You don't think I'm weird or anything?"

"The only ones who are weird are them," said Bolivia firmly.

When DeDe got off the phone, Bolivia immediately called Rory. "Hey," she demanded of him, "why did you turn down DeDe's party invitation?"

"I'm busy that day," said Rory.

"Busy? Doing what?"

"I don't have to tell you everything," Rory said.

"That's true, you don't," said Bolivia. "But I was surprised because I thought you'd be going. And I thought Derek would be going too. And I was already planning how we could make some costumes together."

"Why do you have to go?" Rory asked. "Don't we have enough fun together without DeDe and that friend of hers, Aldo? We could make our own party."

"Go ahead. Make your own party," Bolivia said. "But don't expect me to come. I'm going to

DeDe's party. So there," she told Rory before she hung up the phone.

Bolivia was upset over this turn of events. She wanted very much to get to know more people, but not at the expense of losing Rory and Derek's friendship. Why did they feel she had to choose one friend over another? She didn't even want to go to DeDe's party anymore. But she wouldn't give Rory and Derek the satisfaction of knowing she had backed out. Furthermore, she didn't want to hurt poor DeDe's feelings. It wasn't her fault that the boys were so cliquish.

The next morning, though Rory and Derek walked to the bus stop as usual with Bolivia, there was a feeling of tension among them. Bolivia thought of asking Rory about Eeny. Certainly that was a neutral subject. You couldn't help having warm feelings about the kittens. But then she thought, Why should I make the effort? It was as much Rory and Derek's responsibility to make conversation and to be friendly. So they reached the bus stop without saying anything. Luckily or unluckily it was one of those mornings when there was no double seat available. They separated on the bus and didn't see one another again until dismissal time.

When they met in the afternoon, Rory was smiling. He almost looked as if he had some sort of secret. Whatever it was, it put him in a good mood, and he and Derek joked with Bolivia like old times. They did their homework together over at Rory's house and played with his kitten. But from time to time Bolivia noticed the two boys exchanging glances. It was as if they knew something that they weren't sharing with her.

That evening DeDe phoned again. "The strangest thing happened today," she told Bolivia. "There was a note stuck into my locker. Someone had cut out letters from a magazine and used them to spell the words. I saw it in a movie once."

"What did the note say?"

"'Beware of BR,'" said DeDe. "My Spanish teacher is named Bianca Ruiz. So all during Spanish I kept watching in case something was going to happen. But it was an ordinary class period. Nothing unusual. Then in the afternoon, when I showed the note to Aldo, he pointed out that other people have those same initials."

"People like me," said Bolivia. She had realized

that as soon as DeDe had told her the contents of the note.

"Yeah. So tell me. Should I beware of you?" asked DeDe.

"My parents took me to see Shakespeare's play *Julius Caesar* last spring," said Bolivia. "Caesar gets a warning to beware the ides of March. That means March fifteenth. And sure enough, on that date he gets murdered by some of his friends."

"Great friends!" said DeDe. "What are you planning to do to me?"

"Be your friend. Period. That is, if you aren't afraid of me."

"I'm not afraid." DeDe giggled. "But I thought you should know about my note."

"Thanks," said Bolivia. "I'm glad you told me. Besides, maybe it doesn't even mean me. Do you know any other people with the initials BR?"

"Not offhand, but I'll keep thinking about it," said DeDe.

"Good," said Bolivia. She didn't want to tell DeDe that she was certain that she was indeed the BR that the note referred to. She also had a pretty strong suspicion about who had sent that note. How could Rory and Derek do something so sneaky and rotten? Of course, she couldn't prove it. But *they* had better beware if that was the way they were going to behave.

On Thursday at dismissal time Bolivia bumped into DeDe in the hallway at school. DeDe opened her notebook and showed Bolivia a second note she had just removed from her locker. Like the first, the words were spelled out in letters cut from a magazine: "Say good-bye to Aldoe now that BR has her eyes on him."

Bolivia felt her face turning red. How could Rory and Derek embarrass her this way? "Is that how Aldo spells his name?" she asked, pretending not to understand the meaning of the note.

"There's no *e*," said DeDe. "Listen," she said to Bolivia, "Aldo is my best friend. But he's not my boyfriend. He's just a friend-friend. So I'm not competing with you."

"I like him," admitted Bolivia. "I think he's a neat person. But I'm not looking for a boyfriend. I just want you to know that. And you can tell Aldo that too. But I hope we can all still hang out together even if these stupid notes keep coming."

"Don't worry," said DeDe. "The more notes I

get, the more I remember that I like you. I'm glad you're coming to my party."

"And I'm glad that some other people aren't," said Bolivia pointedly.

DeDe rushed off to catch the bus, and Bolivia went to the music room, where the members of the chorus were gathering. Her pleasure in the music was ruined that afternoon because of her angry thoughts about Rory and Derek. She imagined them at that very moment working on their next note to DeDe.

Leaving the school building with Mr. Dunn at 4:30 P.M., however, Bolivia saw that she had been wrong. The boys hadn't spent the afternoon sitting home and cutting letters out of magazines. But they had done other mischief, and the sight of it made Bolivia furious. Up and down the sidewalk outside the school building were chalked hearts. Inside each big heart was written BR & AS. Bolivia felt like screaming! She turned to look at Rory's father. If he noticed the graffiti, he paid no attention to it.

"How's it going?" he asked Bolivia.

Bolivia knew he'd be shocked if she told him

how things were really going. How his son was sending poison-pen letters about her. How Rory got angry when she wanted to meet other people. How he felt betrayed because she wanted to stay after school one afternoon each week. But since Bolivia was neither a tattletale nor a whiner, she said nothing about what was really on her mind.

"Okay," she lied. But then because she couldn't help herself, she added, "Rory and Derek are stupid not to join any of the afterschool clubs."

"They will," said Mr. Dunn confidently. "They just aren't ready yet. This is a big school, and some kids take longer than others to feel comfortable here after they arrive from their small and cozy elementary schools."

Bolivia shrugged.

Later that evening, after supper, Derek came over to the Goldings' house to give Bolivia's uncle a magazine with a long article about photography. "My father said he thought you'd want to read this," he told Mr. Golding. Derek turned to Bolivia and smiled shyly at her. Bolivia didn't return the smile. She was too angry at Derek and Rory even to pretend otherwise.

"So long," Derek said.

Mr. Golding sat down at once to read the article. "Oh, what a shame," he called out as he turned the page of the article.

"What is it, dear?" Mrs. Golding asked, turning toward her husband. She was in the midst of pinning up the cuffs of a green shirt that Bolivia was going to wear to DeDe's Halloween party.

"Someone cut a hole in the middle of this article," Mr. Golding said. He held up the magazine for his wife to see. "Look, on this page too," he added, showing another page with a hole in it.

Bolivia's face turned red with anger. Not only was the magazine proof that Derek was Rory's accomplice in sending out poison-pen letters, but he was stupid enough to deliver the evidence right to her house.

"Hold still," Aunt Sophie said to Bolivia. "What's gotten into you all of a sudden? You're as skittish as Moe."

"Sorry," said Bolivia. "I couldn't help it. I just thought of something."

"There," said her aunt, sticking the last pin into the sleeve. "You can take the shirt off now. And I'll be able to sew it."

Bolivia pulled the green shirt off. Underneath

was the T-shirt she'd worn to school. She thought about running over to the Curry house and giving Derek a piece of her mind. But then she thought better of it. Maybe she could come up with some clever way of getting back at the boys. So instead she went upstairs to check on Lucette.

Halfway up the stairs she called down to her aunt and uncle, "Do you know what the weather is going to be tomorrow?"

"Pretty much the same as today, I think," said Uncle Lou.

"Too bad," said Bolivia glumly, thinking of the chalk marks in front of the school. "I was hoping for rain."

Dear Mom & Dad,

My friend DeDe invited me to a Halloween party. Rory and Derek were invited too, but they decided not to go. I'm feeling very angry at them at the moment. You wouldn't believe the disgusting things they are capable of doing. They stick together like glue, for better or for worse. Most of the time it's for worse, if you ask me.

Anyhow, I wore a green swimming cap of Aunt Sophie's and a green shirt belonging to Uncle Lou to the party. I made a sort of beak for myself out of paper and tied it around my head with a piece of string. Can you guess what my costume was?

DeDe has a great dog named Cookie. Even she was in costume, with a bandanna around her neck and a cowboy hat on her head. When someone accidentally knocked over a bowl of popcorn, Cookie ate it all up. DeDe calls her a canine vacuum cleaner. It was really funny to see. I never knew that dogs ate popcorn. DeDe says Cookie will eat just about anything, and she does.

Love & hugs,
Bolivia

# 11
# Thanksgiving
# Plans

Maybe it was because of her strained relationship with Rory and Derek. Maybe it was because it was two months since she had last seen her parents. Maybe it had to do with the approach of Thanksgiving. Whatever the reason, at the start of November Bolivia began to feel twinges of homesickness.

Back in Ithaca Bolivia's parents always celebrated the holiday with a large group of friends from the university. They took turns hosting the Thanksgiving meal. Last year there had been seventeen people sitting around the Raabs' dinner table. They had ranged in age from seven months to eighty-one years. Remembering that happy and lively occasion made Bolivia feel sad. She had never eaten Thanksgiving dinner apart from her parents.

Then Bolivia thought of DeDe. She wondered how her friend celebrated holidays, shifting between parents.

"Will you stay home or go away to your father's for Thanksgiving?" Bolivia asked DeDe when she was sitting next to her on the school bus a few days after Halloween.

DeDe made a face. "Last year I had the holiday with my mother, so I thought for sure I was going to be with my father this year. But it looks like he is spending the weekend with his latest girlfriend at the ski house they rented in Vermont. I guess I'll be staying home. What do they need me for?" DeDe asked, shrugging. "Last year my mother and I ate out in a restaurant," she added. "It turned out better than I thought. And it saved my mother the work."

"Last year my mother cooked a twenty-five-pound turkey," said Bolivia. "Now she's *in* Turkey." She sighed. She was sorry that she had reminded DeDe about her parents' divorce. Usually DeDe was so upbeat, but whenever she spoke about her parents' marital situation, she grew unhappy.

"I guess you must miss your parents," DeDe commented. "It's bad enough that sometimes I only see my dad once a month. At least I've got my mother. And Cookie," she added.

"I've got an idea," said Bolivia suddenly.

"What is it?" asked DeDe.

"I can't tell you yet. It may not work out. But maybe it will," said Bolivia hopefully. She couldn't wait for the school day to end so she could discuss her idea with her aunt and uncle.

"Could we invite DeDe and her mother to have Thanksgiving dinner with us?" Bolivia asked them at supper that night. "I'll help you fix everything. I helped my mother last year. I was in charge of the turkey stuffing."

"Oh, dear." Mrs. Golding looked distressed by Bolivia's unexpected question. "Your uncle and I don't even know DeDe's mother. We've only met DeDe a couple of times. They probably wouldn't want to spend a family holiday with us."

"We could ask," said Bolivia. "That is, if you're willing. DeDe told me that last year she and her mother ate their dinner at a restaurant."

"In a restaurant?" Aunt Sophie said thoughtfully. "That's too bad."

"I think it stinks," said Bolivia. "And since there's only three of us and two of them, I think we should celebrate together."

"Maybe DeDe's mother has made other plans that you don't know about," suggested Aunt Sophie. "Besides," she added, "a few weeks ago Mrs. Dunn hinted that maybe we could join their family for the holiday meal. She hasn't actually asked us yet. But I have a feeling that she will."

Bolivia made a face. There was no way she wanted to spend the holiday with Rory. Even though he and Derek hadn't sent any more poison-pen notes to DeDe in the past few days, she hadn't forgiven them for their past actions. Her relationship with them had certainly cooled off. She refused to do homework with them after school, and she was already trying to think of an excuse not to spend the coming Saturday with them either. She didn't want to spend her time with such sneaky, mean-spirited guys as they had become of late.

"Could I phone DeDe and find out what they're

planning?" asked Bolivia. "The Dunns and the Currys have each other. But DeDe and her mother are alone." The more she thought about celebrating the holiday with DeDe and her mother, the better she liked the idea.

"What do you think, Lou?" Mrs. Golding asked, turning to her husband.

"I think if Bolivia wants to invite some friends, we should let her. People who haven't eaten your pumpkin pie don't know what a treat there is in store for them."

Bolivia grinned as Aunt Sophie smiled at the compliment. Her great-aunt was an excellent cook. But the truth was that even though food was a big part of the Thanksgiving celebration, it was also about sharing.

To Bolivia's delight, DeDe and her mother accepted the invitation. "This is so kind of you," Mrs. Rawson kept saying, first to Bolivia and then to Mrs. Golding when she spoke to her.

"It sounds like I'm going traveling." DeDe giggled into the phone. "Wait till I announce to my father that I'm going to Bolivia for Thanksgiving."

"DeDe's mother seems like a lovely person," Aunt Sophie commented when the telephone call was concluded. "She was so pleasant on the phone. That was a very generous idea you had to invite them here."

"It was generous of you to agree," said Bolivia, giving her aunt a hug. Then she picked up Moe and gave the kitten a happy squeeze too.

Bolivia didn't mention to Rory and Derek that DeDe was coming to have Thanksgiving dinner on Dogleg Lane. The trio hardly spoke at all as they walked to the bus the next morning. Derek attempted to start a conversation, but neither Rory nor Bolivia gave much response to his comments.

A few evenings later Mrs. Dunn phoned and formally invited the Goldings and Bolivia to join her family at the holiday meal. "I explained to her that we had made other plans," said Mrs. Golding when she got off the phone. "At first I thought the Dunns and Currys could come over here for dessert, but she told me that they were going to have fourteen people at their table. So we both decided it wouldn't work out."

"Right," said Bolivia, nodding. She wondered if her aunt had any idea of how angry she felt toward Rory and Derek these days.

About ten minutes later the phone rang for the

second time that evening. This time the call was for Bolivia. It was Derek.

"Yes?" said Bolivia, wondering what he wanted from her.

"I just had a call from Rory," he said. "He's really disappointed that you aren't going to his house for Thanksgiving."

"They're going to have a load of other people," Bolivia said. "He doesn't need me. He'll have you."

"No, he won't. My parents and I always go away for Thanksgiving weekend," Derek explained.

"Oh," said Bolivia, surprised. She didn't think Derek ever went anywhere without Rory. "Well, we made other plans too."

"Where are you going?" Derek asked.

"Nowhere. We invited DeDe and her mother to come here."

"And what about Aldo?" asked Derek.

"What about him?"

"Isn't he coming too?" Derek wanted to know.

"Why would you think that? I hardly know him. And he has his own family," said Bolivia.

"Well, you hardly know DeDe. And she has

her own family," Derek pointed out.

Bolivia looked over her shoulder to see if her aunt and uncle were listening. Luckily they seemed absorbed in a television program they were watching in the next room.

"Look, Derek, I don't know what's wrong with you and Rory. It doesn't make sense for you to keep being so jealous of DeDe and Aldo. I like them. I want to get to know DeDe better. Maybe I'll get to know Aldo better. But that doesn't mean you and Rory had to get so unpleasant and so unreasonable. You missed a great party at DeDe's home. But the way you've both been acting lately, sending poison-pen letters and stuff, I was really glad that you weren't there." Bolivia stopped to catch her breath.

"I told Rory it was a stupid thing to do," said Derek, defending himself.

"Don't blame Rory. You're just as guilty as he is. I saw the magazine you brought over here for my uncle to read. It was full of mysterious holes. Only it didn't take Sherlock Holmes to solve the mystery. BR was able to do it one-two-three. I don't know how you could do something like that."

"I'm sorry," said Derek. "It was pretty awful.

But after all, you're supposed to be our special friend," he said.

"Of course I'm your special friend. That is, I *used* to be your friend. You're the first people I got to know in Woodside, after Aunt Sophie and Uncle Lou. And you've been to visit at my house in Ithaca. But that doesn't mean you can expect me not to talk to other people and not to make other friends while I'm here," Bolivia said angrily.

"Do you like Aldo?" Derek asked.

"What do you mean, do I like Aldo? Sure I like him. He's a nice person. He helped me with the kittens. He's interesting, and he's different. I like him a lot."

"I thought so," said Derek.

"You thought what?" asked Bolivia.

"I thought you were in love with him."

"Love?" Bolivia's voice rose with surprise. "What are you talking about? Who said anything about *love*? I'm not in love with *anyone*. You've been watching too many dopey TV programs," she said.

"You mean you're not in love with him?" asked Derek, sounding relieved.

"Derek Curry, I'm not even twelve years old.

Why should I be in love with anyone?" Bolivia said.

"I don't know. Rory and I were talking about it, and he said you had a thing for Aldo."

"I don't have a *thing* for anyone or anything," said Bolivia. She banged down the telephone in disgust.

Bolivia went upstairs and thought about Derek's disturbing phone call as she cleaned out Lucette's cage. She had never known boys could act so stupid. In fact, although she had originally thought she'd get back at Rory and Derek, she had quickly changed her mind. Sure she could send them some poison-pen letters or chalk up messages about them or even come up with some other hurtful action, but that would be behaving just as ridiculously and immaturely as they were.

A few minutes later, while Bolivia was in the midst of changing the water for Lucette, Mrs. Golding called to her.

"Bolivia, Derek's here. He wants to come up and talk to you."

"All right," Bolivia called down. What does he want now? she wondered.

Derek's face, which flushed easily when he

was embarrassed, was redder than Bolivia had ever seen it. Even his ears were bright red. "I've got to ask you something very important," he said.

"Go ahead," said Bolivia. She kept her back to him as she put the little cup of fresh water into Lucette's cage.

"You said you're not in love with Aldo, right?" asked Derek.

"Right," agreed Bolivia.

"Well, I don't know how you feel about me. But I just wanted to tell you that I like you a whole lot, and I hope that when we grow up, you'll marry me," Derek said.

"What?" Bolivia turned around to look at Derek.

"I just wanted to ask you before Aldo or some other kid does," he said.

"Are you crazy?" asked Bolivia, blushing at the unexpected words.

"Yeah," admitted Derek. "I'm crazy about you. And I'd really like it if we got married when we're old enough."

"Derek Curry, you can't propose marriage to

someone when you're in sixth grade." She giggled nervously.

"Why not?" Derek wanted to know.

"Because—because I'm in sixth grade too. We have two and a half years of middle school and then four years of high school and then four years of college and maybe more school after that. Who knows what we'll want to do ten and a half years from now? We're only eleven years old, for heaven's sake."

"Eleven and a half. Almost eleven and three-quarters," said Derek.

"Did you discuss this with Rory? Does he know you're asking me this?" Bolivia demanded.

"Do you want to marry him instead?" asked Derek, looking very disappointed.

"Derek, I don't want to marry *anybody*."

"Well, you don't have to make your mind up now," Derek said. "I didn't talk about this with Rory. It's personal," he pointed out.

"You mean you actually thought of something on your own?" asked Bolivia. She couldn't help being surprised. And flattered. "Listen," she said to Derek, "if you still want to marry me ten years from now, you can ask me then. Okay?"

"Okay," Derek said. "But remember, I asked you first."

"Don't worry," said Bolivia. "I'll never forget."

☼ — DAY

2  R+ 🛶 +Y,

u     K+ ☃ –S        👁

🛋 – L P     y+ 🛶     🪣 – i .

🛑     🐝 + 💍 – R     D+ ☝ – TH .

South America

# 12
# The Holiday Dinner

At least once a week since September, Bolivia had written a letter to her parents. Some weeks, when there was something especially exciting, like the discovery of the kittens, she had written two letters. But the note she wrote to Rory took more time than writing *three* letters. It took more time and energy than an evening with math + social studies + German homework. Still, she felt good when she finally completed it. Unlike Rory, and the letters he'd sent to DeDe, she'd signed it. She'd given a clear clue to her name, so she was pretty sure he'd understand that. Instead of sticking it in his locker or handing it to him, she put it in an envelope and posted it in the mailbox on the corner. Their friendship was worth much more

147

than the price of a postage stamp to her.

Bolivia didn't ask Rory if he got her letter. And Rory didn't mention that he'd gotten it. But she was sure he had. The question was, Did he get the message?

On Thanksgiving morning Aunt Sophie put the turkey in the oven even before breakfast. Uncle Lou went outside to pick up the newspaper from the walk. He returned two minutes later with the paper and some news that wasn't in it.

"I just saw Dr. Curry," he reported. "It seems their car started making strange noises as they were driving last night, and he decided it would be wiser to return home than continue their trip and risk breaking down."

"What about Thanksgiving?" asked Aunt Sophie.

"What about it?" her husband wanted to know.

"Where are they going to eat their dinner? We could invite them to come here." Mrs. Golding rushed to the phone.

Bolivia realized that her aunt was going to invite Derek and his parents to come to their house for the holiday meal. She hoped Mrs. Curry had already spoken to Mrs. Dunn. Bolivia worried that it would be a setback to her relationship with Rory if Derek wound up eating turkey at the Goldings' instead of at the Dunns'. Rory would think she had arranged it.

"It's all settled," said Aunt Sophie, returning from the phone and beaming with delight. "They're coming here. I'm glad I bought a large bird." She opened the oven to check on how the turkey was doing.

After breakfast Bolivia helped her aunt cut up vegetables. The kitchen already smelled like Thanksgiving. The aroma was one of the best parts of the holiday, Bolivia thought. That and being together with people you loved. She wondered what her parents were doing just then. She looked at her watch. It was almost nine-thirty in the morning. That made it four-thirty in the afternoon in Turkey—almost time for dinner. But it wasn't a holiday there.

When there was nothing left that needed doing, Bolivia went to the phone. Better call and get it over with, she thought. She dialed Rory's number.

"Hi," she said when he answered the phone. "Let's take a walk. Just the two of us. I want to talk to you."

Rory looked very glum when he met Bolivia in front of the house a couple of minutes later.

"I guess you heard that Derek's coming to have dinner with me today," she said.

"Yeah," said Rory angrily. "It's not fair. He should be coming to my house."

"He *should* be in New Hope, Pennsylvania. He couldn't help it if they had car trouble. And he couldn't help it that my aunt found out and invited him and his parents to eat with us."

"Yeah, sure," said Rory.

"Boy, are you stupid!" Bolivia said. "He's still your best friend. So he eats dinner in someone else's house. So what? Why are you so possessive and so jealous all the time?" she yelled at Rory.

"I'm not possessive or jealous," Rory shouted back.

"Right. And the American flag is green, yellow, and purple," said Bolivia.

They walked along the street without talking for a couple of minutes.

"Did you get my letter?" Bolivia asked Rory.

"Yeah," said Rory. "You're not very good at drawing."

"I know, but I really meant what I said in it. If you're going to act so dumb about things, I won't be your friend."

"Who's dumb?" asked Rory. "I just got all A's on my report card, and you know it."

"Big deal," said Bolivia. "So did I, but that's not what I mean. You're dumb about other things that you don't get graded for on your report card."

"If that's the way you feel about me, I don't need you for a friend either." Rory tried to shout at Bolivia, but his voice cracked. He turned around and started back toward his house.

Bolivia reached out and grabbed Rory by the jacket. "Listen to me for a minute," she said, softening her tone. She realized Rory was close to tears. "This should be such a special time. Here I am spending all these weeks in Woodside, and instead of us having great times together, you're busy writing poison-pen notes and chalking stupid messages about me on the sidewalk and acting weird."

"Yeah. Well, how can we have great times together if you're always running around with DeDe and Aldo?" Rory asked.

"I don't spend all my time with them. But you can't expect me to spend every minute with you either. You can't put me in a cage like Lucette and make me wait till you decide what we're going to do. Today I'm having dinner with DeDe and Derek. Tomorrow you and I could be doing something together. But it's up to you."

"Most likely you'll be eating leftover turkey tomorrow with DeDe or Aldo or someone," Rory grumbled.

"Listen," said Bolivia, "in case you don't know it, Aldo is a vegetarian, so he won't be eating any leftover turkey with me or with anyone else. But that's not the point. You're silly not to let yourself get to know him better. You don't let yourself get to know anyone but Derek and me. That's just plain dumb. I bet there are loads of kids in the middle school who you'd like if you got to know them."

"So what?" said Rory. "I've got Derek. I don't need them. And I don't need you."

"Do you mean that?" asked Bolivia. She let go

of Rory's jacket, which she'd been holding on to all this time, and backed away.

Rory was silent for a moment. "No," he said softly. "You're my second best friend. At least you used to be. Can't we still be friends?" he asked.

"Sure," said Bolivia. "But you have to let me make other friends too."

They started walking again. Then Rory said something that surprised Bolivia. "I called Aldo on the phone," he said.

"You did?" she asked, amazed.

"Yeah. Eeny scratched Edna last night, and my mother got all upset. She said we might have to give her away. So I called Aldo to ask his advice. He knows so much about cats and kittens."

"What did he say?" Bolivia asked.

"He's going to come over to my house tomorrow and show me how to trim Eeny's claws with a nail clipper. He says it's easy once you know how to do it."

"That's great," said Bolivia. "Can I join you? I'm worried about Aunt Sophie's sofa. I saw Moe clawing at it a couple of times."

"Sure," Rory said.

When the two friends reached the intersection

that would have brought them into the center of town, they turned around and began to retrace their steps.

"Guess what?" said Rory.

"What?" asked Bolivia. If Rory had actually phoned Aldo, there was no telling what other surprise he had in store for her.

"I decided that I'm going to join the staff of the school magazine."

"You are?" asked Bolivia in amazement. "That's great."

"Yeah. My English teacher's been after me. She says I have a lot of talent. She's been saying good things about my writing ever since school started."

"I'm not surprised," said Bolivia. "You do write well. I always looked forward to the letters you sent me when I was in Ithaca."

"You did?" asked Rory, looking pleased.

"Yes. I like the letters where you sign your name," said Bolivia. "I don't like your poison-pen letters, though."

Rory blushed. "Yeah. Derek told me how you figured out that we did that. I didn't think you'd find out."

"So what made you change your mind about

the school magazine?" asked Bolivia, going back to the happier subject.

"Well, at first I didn't want to join the magazine because my father's the faculty adviser," Rory explained. "I thought everyone would think he'd print anything I wrote because I'm his son. But he told me that the students vote on what gets printed."

Bolivia nodded her head. "What about Derek? Is he also going to join?" she asked.

"No," Rory said. "He really doesn't like to write if he can avoid it."

"Well, there are so many afterschool clubs that I bet he could find something he likes. You guys don't have to cling to each other all the time like Siamese twins."

"Yeah," Rory said. "I guess you're right. He wanted me to go cross-country racing with him. But his legs are so much longer than mine that I could never keep up with him."

Bolivia agreed.

"I've got this great idea of doing interviews with students for the magazine," Rory said. "Each one would be just a few paragraphs long. It would help everyone get to know one another better. Our school's so huge that there are loads of kids we might have things in common with, but we'll never even be in the same class with them."

"That's a neat idea," Bolivia said approvingly.

"I thought I'd do the first interview with Aldo," Rory said. "I bet he's not the only vegetarian in the school. If there are others, they'd want to get to know him."

"You're absolutely right," said Bolivia enthusiastically. She was just about to ask Rory if she could hang out with him when he interviewed Aldo. But she realized that such a suggestion would defeat her plan of encouraging Rory to do things on his own. She'd just have to wait and read the interview when it was published.

A car filled with passengers pulled up alongside them, and a window opened. "Rory!" a woman's voice called out.

Rory turned his head to look. "Hey, Aunt Mona," he called. He turned to Bolivia. "Looks like my relatives are coming already."

"Meet you at the house," his aunt called to Rory.

"If you have dinner earlier than we do, maybe you can come over to my aunt's afterward," suggested Bolivia as they walked back toward Dogleg Lane.

"Great," said Rory. "And listen," he said, "about those notes. Well, I'm sorry."

"That's okay, it's over," said Bolivia. "You just got carried away. It must be from watching too much TV."

"Didn't you watch that nature program that Aldo told you about?" asked Rory. "Not all TV is bad."

"You're right," Bolivia said. "I've actually watched several other nature shows in that series. There was a terrific one on snakes a couple of nights ago. I guess I have to be more open to television and not be such a snob about it."

"See you later," Rory called when they reached his door.

About seven hours later, after Rory's Thanksgiving company had all departed, he arrived at the Goldings' house just in time for dessert.

Bolivia set a place for him. "What can I offer you?" asked Bolivia's aunt, pointing to the various pies on the table.

"Try the pecan pie," suggested DeDe. "My mother made it."

"My mother made the apple crumb," said Derek. "It's great, and it's from the last of the apples that we picked." He looked over at Mrs. Golding and added, "But the pumpkin pie is awfully good too."

"Take a little of each," said Bolivia. She realized that by making a choice, Rory might offend one of the pie makers.

"Why a little?" asked Rory. "I want big pieces of each one."

"Good for you," said Uncle Lou.

Bolivia slid the plate with the pumpkin pie over toward Rory. He had an amazing appetite for a kid his size. He'd probably wake up one morning and discover that he'd suddenly doubled in height overnight.

"It's really nice that we're all here together," said DeDe happily. "The only one missing is Aldo."

Bolivia noticed that her friend didn't mention the fact that her father was absent from the gathering. She guessed that meant that DeDe was satisfied with the company around her and didn't miss him—at least for the moment. Bolivia smiled at DeDe. She hoped Rory and Derek had finally resolved their jealousy of her new friends. By doing so, they had made some new friends for themselves as well. It should have been enough to make her feel thankful. But for her something was still missing today.

She felt something moving down at her feet and bent to look under the table. There was Moe, playing with the laces on her sneakers.

"I bet Moe would love some turkey," she said.

At the very moment that the word *turkey* left her mouth, the telephone rang.

"Who can that be?" Uncle Lou wondered aloud as he went to answer it. A smile crossed his face as he heard the voice on the other end.

"Bolivia," he shouted, "come quickly. It's for you!"

Bolivia jumped up so fast that she knocked her chair over onto the floor and her glass of milk onto the table. There could only be two people calling her today. "Hello!" she shouted into the phone.

"Bolivia. Happy Thanksgiving. Tell me. How are you?" her mother's voice asked. The connection was fuzzy, and there was a slight echo to the

words. Still, it was so good to hear her mother's voice that tears welled up in Bolivia's eyes. She swallowed hard before she began speaking. She didn't want her mother to know she was crying.

"I'm fine," said Bolivia.

"How are things going, honey?" her mother asked.

"Everything's great," Bolivia said. "Did you get my letter about Aunt Sophie and Uncle Lou letting me keep Moe? And I joined the chorus. I found out I'm a soprano. We're going to be in a concert together with the choral society from the high school. And I've made some new friends besides Rory and Derek. My friend DeDe is here right now with her mother for Thanksgiving dinner. And Rory and Derek are here too." Bolivia paused to catch her breath. "I'm talking too much." She giggled. "Tell me about you and Dad."

"I'm putting Dad on now," her mother said. "He has some good news for you."

"Honey, how are you?" Bolivia's father asked.

"Great, Dad. How are you?"

"We're absolutely fine here. But we've missed

you so much and worried whether everything was going well for you. So we've arranged to come to Woodside to spend the week between Christmas and New Year's with you and Aunt Sophie and Uncle Lou. How does that sound?" he asked her.

"Oh, Dad, that's super," Bolivia shouted into the phone.

"And if you want to come back with us to Turkey until we finish our project in April, you could even do that. It won't kill you to miss a bit of school. We could get the assignments and the books, and you could study here."

"Oh, Dad," said Bolivia, startled by this sudden possibility. She looked at her aunt and uncle and her friends sitting around the table. She didn't know if she'd be ready to leave them all so soon.

"You don't have to make up your mind now," her father said. "And whatever you decide is fine. But we wanted to give you that option. All right?"

"All right," Bolivia said.

"Mom wants to talk to you some more," her father said. "Keep sending those letters, honey. We love getting them."

"Darling, we send you a thousand, thousand

kisses," Mrs. Raab told Bolivia when she spoke again to her. "We'll be seeing you before you know it. Now let me speak to Aunt Sophie," she requested.

"What time is it there?" Aunt Sophie asked into the telephone.

Bolivia looked down at her watch. It was almost 6:00 in the evening in Woodside. That meant it was way past midnight in Turkey. Her parents had to stay up late in order to place their call. She sat back down at the table. Suddenly she had much more of an appetite for all the food around her. She reached for the pies.

She turned to see if Rory noticed that she was having three slices of pie, just as he had. But he was busy talking to DeDe and didn't seem aware of her for the moment.

Bolivia had a feeling that she wouldn't be ready to say good-bye at the end of the next month. She thought she'd even like to finish out the school year here in Woodside. But she didn't have to make up her mind about that right now. Now all she had to decide was which pie to bite into first.

"Hey, Bolivia, there's one thing I always wondered about," said Derek.

"What's that?" asked Bolivia, chewing a mouthful of pumpkin pie.

"Do the people in Turkey eat a lot of turkey?"

Bolivia shrugged as everyone around the table laughed.